OPPOSING
VIEWPOINTS®
SERIES

The Middle Class

DATE DUE

3/8/18	

Other Books of Related Interest:

Opposing Viewpoints Series

American Values

Consumerism

Welfare

At Issue Series

Do Tax Breaks Benefit the Economy?

Gay and Lesbian Families

Reality TV

Current Controversies Series

Consumer Debt

Family Violence

The Wage Gap

"Congress shall make no law . . . abridging the freedom of speech, or of the press."

First Amendment to the U.S. Constitution

The basic foundation of our democracy is the First Amendment guarantee of freedom of expression. The Opposing Viewpoints Series is dedicated to the concept of this basic freedom and the idea that it is more important to practice it than to enshrine it.

**OPPOSING
VIEWPOINTS®
SERIES**

The Middle Class

*David Haugen, Susan Musser, and Vickey Kalambakal,
Book Editors*

GREENHAVEN PRESS
A part of Gale, Cengage Learning

GALE
CENGAGE Learning·

Detroit • New York • San Francisco • New Haven, Conn • Waterville, Maine • London

GALE
CENGAGE Learning

Christine Nasso, *Publisher*
Elizabeth Des Chenes, *Managing Editor*

For more information, contact:
Greenhaven Press
27500 Drake Rd.
Farmington Hills, MI 48331-3535
Or you can visit our Internet site at gale.cengage.com

Articles in Greenhaven Press anthologies are often edited for length to meet page requirements. In addition, original titles of these works are changed to clearly present the main thesis and to explicitly indicate the author's opinion. Every effort is made to ensure that Greenhaven Press accurately reflects the original intent of the authors. Every effort has been made to trace the owners of copyrighted material.

Cover photograph © IoFoto/Dreamstime.com.

LIBRARY OF CONGRESS CATALOGING-IN-PUBLICATION DATA

The middle class / David Haugen, Susan Musser, and Vickey Kalambakal, book editors.
    p. cm. -- (Opposing viewpoints)
    Includes bibliographical references and index.
    ISBN 978-0-7377-4777-5 (hbk.) -- ISBN 978-0-7377-4778-2 (pbk.)
    1. Middle class--United States--Juvenile literature. I. Haugen, David M., 1969- II. Musser, Susan. III. Kalambakal, Vickey.
    HT690.U6M47 2010
    305.5'50973--dc22

                                    2009049023

Printed in the United States of America

Contents

Chapter 3: What Is the Status of Minorities in America's Middle Class?

Why Consider Opposing Viewpoints?

> *"The only way in which a human being can make some approach to knowing the whole of a subject is by hearing what can be said about it by persons of every variety of opinion and studying all modes in which it can be looked at by every character of mind. No wise man ever acquired his wisdom in any mode but this."*
>
> John Stuart Mill

In our media-intensive culture it is not difficult to find differing opinions. Thousands of newspapers and magazines and dozens of radio and television talk shows resound with differing points of view. The difficulty lies in deciding which opinion to agree with and which "experts" seem the most credible. The more inundated we become with differing opinions and claims, the more essential it is to hone critical reading and thinking skills to evaluate these ideas. Opposing Viewpoints books address this problem directly by presenting stimulating debates that can be used to enhance and teach these skills. The varied opinions contained in each book examine many different aspects of a single issue. While examining these conveniently edited opposing views, readers can develop critical thinking skills such as the ability to compare and contrast authors' credibility, facts, argumentation styles, use of persuasive techniques, and other stylistic tools. In short, the Opposing Viewpoints Series is an ideal way to attain the higher-level thinking and reading skills so essential in a culture of diverse and contradictory opinions.

In addition to providing a tool for critical thinking, Opposing Viewpoints books challenge readers to question their own strongly held opinions and assumptions. Most people form their opinions on the basis of upbringing, peer pressure, and personal, cultural, or professional bias. By reading carefully balanced opposing views, readers must directly confront new ideas as well as the opinions of those with whom they disagree. This is not to argue simplistically that everyone who reads opposing views will—or should—change his or her opinion. Instead, the series enhances readers' understanding of their own views by encouraging confrontation with opposing ideas. Careful examination of others' views can lead to the readers' understanding of the logical inconsistencies in their own opinions, perspective on why they hold an opinion, and the consideration of the possibility that their opinion requires further evaluation.

Evaluating Other Opinions

To ensure that this type of examination occurs, Opposing Viewpoints books present all types of opinions. Prominent spokespeople on different sides of each issue as well as well-known professionals from many disciplines challenge the reader. An additional goal of the series is to provide a forum for other, less known, or even unpopular viewpoints. The opinion of an ordinary person who has had to make the decision to cut off life support from a terminally ill relative, for example, may be just as valuable and provide just as much insight as a medical ethicist's professional opinion. The editors have two additional purposes in including these less known views. One, the editors encourage readers to respect others' opinions—even when not enhanced by professional credibility. It is only by reading or listening to and objectively evaluating others' ideas that one can determine whether they are worthy of consideration. Two, the inclusion of such viewpoints encourages the important critical thinking skill of objectively evaluating an author's credentials and bias. This evaluation will illuminate an author's reasons for taking a particular stance on an issue and will aid in readers' evaluation of the author's ideas.

It is our hope that these books will give readers a deeper understanding of the issues debated and an appreciation of the complexity of even seemingly simple issues when good and honest people disagree. This awareness is particularly important in a democratic society such as ours in which people enter into public debate to determine the common good. Those with whom one disagrees should not be regarded as enemies but rather as people whose views deserve careful examination and may shed light on one's own.

Thomas Jefferson once said that "difference of opinion leads to inquiry, and inquiry to truth." Jefferson, a broadly educated man, argued that "if a nation expects to be ignorant and free . . . it expects what never was and never will be." As individuals and as a nation, it is imperative that we consider the opinions of others and examine them with skill and discernment. The Opposing Viewpoints Series is intended to help readers achieve this goal.

David L. Bender and Bruno Leone,
Founders

Introduction

> "Quite simply, a strong middle class equals a strong America. We can't have one without the other."
>
> Joseph Biden,
> vice president of the United States,
> January 30, 2009

> "I just hope we're still at least slightly sympathetic to the notion that the American ideal is blind as to economic classes and grounded in equal opportunity for all. Obama's endless appeals to the middle class contradict his promises not to be divisive and to restore unity to America."
>
> David Limbaugh,
> conservative political commentator,
> August 11, 2009

In January 2009, newly elected president Barack Obama established the Middle Class Task Force (MCTF). He tapped his vice president, former senator Joe Biden, to chair the task force, which has been given the job of improving the standard of living for the middle class in the wake of the 2008 financial crisis.

Concerned over falling housing prices, overextended credit, mounting debt, and rising unemployment, Obama intended for the task force to bring together leaders of industry, policy makers, labor unions, and community advocacy groups to find solutions to these problems or at least to lessen their impact on working Americans. "The strength of our economy can be measured by the strength of our middle class," Obama stated at the outset of his term, indicating that his strategy to jump-start the nation's sluggish economy will have much to do with bolstering the middle class and its traditionally strong buying power.

According to Obama's plan, the state of America's middle class can be bettered by improving the lot of organized labor, which many critics say had experienced an erosion of rights and a loss of bargaining power under the Republican administration of George W. Bush. "You cannot have a strong middle class without a strong labor movement," Obama remarked as he signed new orders to strengthen collective bargaining power and facilitate the employment of union labor in federal contracts. Obama and Biden also hope that middle-class recovery might be given a boost by investing in green jobs, which, as CBS News claims, "are more likely to be union jobs." Green jobs are typically employment opportunities in technologies that benefit humans and the environment. CBS reports that the new administration favors these jobs not only for their environmentally friendly aspects but also because they are not usually outsourced overseas. The first meeting of the Middle Class Task Force took up the issue of green job growth. Chris Chafe, executive director of Change to Win, and Van Jones, president of Green For All—two spokespersons who took part in that initial meeting—later said,

> The U.S. economy once abounded with opportunities for careers that would support a family, provide health care, put kids through college, even allow people to take a hard-earned vacation with their loved ones. Those opportunities, and the American dream that propelled generations to new progress, remain too far out of reach for too many Americans. The best place to recreate them is in the growing green jobs sector.

Other politicians and commentators support this emphasis on labor and green technology, but not everyone sees a clear link to helping the middle class.

The administration's critics are quick to point out what they believe are the weaknesses of the middle-class rescue plan. Conservative radio personality Rush Limbaugh maintains that because union workers represent a small percentage of the middle class, promoting organized labor will have little effect on the economy. "The middle class is not organized labor," Limbaugh told his audience in January 2009, contending that unions are looking for "benefits galore, health care and all of that" from a sympathetic administration. Joel Kotkin, who writes a column for *Forbes*, is also skeptical of the president's strategy. Kotkin states that green jobs make up less than 0.5 percent of the nation's total employment. In an August 2009 article, he cites a study by the New America Foundation that concludes, "for the most part, green jobs constitute a negligible factor in employment—and will continue to do so for the foreseeable future." Kotkin goes on to claim that green corporations—especially energy producers—are granted large government subsidies to maintain their competitiveness. These subsidies, Kotkin argues, are a boon for green businesses, but are unfair to their nonsubsidized counterparts, who often must cut back on employment to keep pace. Kotkin cites another study that examined renewable energy subsidies and their effect on the Spanish economy. According to that research, Kotkin writes, "for every 'green' job created more than two were lost in the nonsubsidized economy." Although Kotkin believes that environmentally friendly products and services can play a part in America's future, the economy cannot be spurred, in his opinion, by a rush to embrace green technologies.

Some of Obama's critics believe that the president's policies are a direct assault on the middle class. Floyd and Mary Beth Brown, columnists for the Zanesville, Ohio, *Times Recorder*, claim that the administration's universal health care plan will involve a new tax on the middle class. They also argue that Obama's push for green energy and lower carbon emissions nationwide will force middle class homeowners to spend extra money for home improvements to meet the new federal standards. "Future taxpayers are going to have to pay for all these programs," the Browns insist, "and the middle class will end up shouldering the load."

Underlying all this debate, however, is the tacit assumption that the White House and its host of critics and supporters can delineate the middle class as a quantifiable slice of American society. Barack Obama clearly defined wealthy America as households earning more than $250,000 per year in announcing that these households would bear tax increases. At the same time, he claimed that those households making under $150,000 would receive a tax cut. As some critics have pointed out, though, $250,000 might mean rich in Boise, Idaho, but middle class in New York City.

Experts commonly give a range of incomes to indicate middle class: A 2007 Congressional Research Service report placed the middle class between incomes of $19,000 and $91,000. Jared Bernstein, chief economist and economic policy adviser to the vice president, wrote on the Web site for the Middle Class Task Force: "The Census Bureau tells us that the median household income—the income of the household smack in the middle of the income scale—is about $50,000, so that's certainly got to be considered a middle-class income." More exacting information, he argued, is not as useful to policy makers as coping with the dire predicaments faced by the middle class. "My boss, the vice president, often describes the 'middle class' as any family that can't afford to miss more than two or three paychecks without financial difficulty," Bernstein reported.

If the middle class is difficult to define, then debates over middle-class policy making are bound to be contentious. *Opposing Viewpoints: The Middle Class* examines some of these points of contention as various politicians, spokespersons, and commentators put forth their views on the state of the middle class in America and the problems that may be threatening its security. In chapters that ask, "What Is the State of the Middle Class in America?" "How Do Middle-Class Values Impact Society?" "What Is the Status of Minorities in America's Middle Class?" and "Is the American Middle Class in Decline?" these authors use their own measures of middle-class living to address the current and future progress of this vital part of the nation's economy. But the pundits and analysts have little control over policy making; the responsibility for renewing the middle class or perhaps leaving it to its own devices rests with the president and his staff.

OPPOSING
VIEWPOINTS®
SERIES

CHAPTER 1

What Is the State of the Middle Class in America?

Chapter Preface

Income would seem to be a straightforward indicator of class; however, in the case of the American middle class, this measure often creates more confusion than clarity. Economists generally agree that incomes between $25,000 and $95,000 a year constitute a middle class standard of living. Critics of this range have argued, though, that a household bringing in an amount at the low end of the range does not have much in common with those earning salaries at the higher end. For example, in a 2005 article in the *Christian Science Monitor*, Dante Chinni noted that people living off $25,000 per year simply cannot afford the same commodities possessed by a person earning $95,000. To illustrate his point, he sarcastically quipped, "Ah yes, there's a group of people bound to run into each other while house-hunting."

The debate over what income places an individual in the middle class intensified during the 2008 presidential elections with each candidate attempting to prove that his or her policies would best serve this vaguely defined class. An annual income of $250,000 became a significant marker following Barack Obama's declaration that households with annual earnings above this point would not qualify for his tax cuts because they were clearly among the nation's wealthiest. Pundits on national news programs and editorials nationwide pounced on this figure, pointing out the differences in lifestyle that $250,000 a year could offer an individual living in Manhattan versus an individual living in a city like Abilene, Texas, or Paducah, Kentucky. American citizens with annual incomes of $250,000 or more decried their categorization as wealthy, contending that even though they earned more than 95 percent of all other Americans, they were feeling just as middle class and financially vulnerable as those making one tenth of their income. But Obama's platform to strengthen the middle class clearly did not include extending aid to what his campaign defined as the well-to-do.

The many Americans in the $250,000 income bracket who strongly believe they are middle class are not alone in that belief. Polls routinely find that Americans of all income brackets are likely to define themselves as middle class. Generally these polls find that somewhere around 90 percent of Americans place themselves in the middle class, often with only 1–2 percent claiming upper class status and the remaining 5–7 percent placing themselves in the lower class. Census data has even shown that the percentage of individuals who consider themselves poor accounts for only half of the population occupying the lowest income bracket. Making policy to benefit the middle class, then, would seem far more challenging given that making arbitrary cutoffs will alienate millions of Americans who may not fall within the income range, but still believe themselves to be middle class.

The elasticity of the definition of the middle class can be attributed to a variety of factors, from financial circumstances to a desire to be a part of, or appeal to, an idealized, hardworking, classless America. Taking finances and financial security as measures of the middle class, though, the authors in the following chapter discuss the state of the middle class in the United States and whether the ethics of these individuals are changing as the country experiences tough times economically.

> *"The idea that the middle class is burdened by unprecedented amounts of debt—that people are borrowing to make ends meet—is overstated."*

The Middle Class Possesses Luxuries, Job Security, and Little Credit Card Debt

Clive Crook

In the viewpoint that follows, Clive Crook examines the recent emphasis on class divisions in the United States, comparing it to the relative classlessness that he sees in British society today. He argues that claims of increasing debt and job insecurity within the American middle class have been exaggerated in recent years by politicians hoping to secure the favor and votes of the middle class, a group into which most voting Americans fall. While he does admit that the middle class faces some challenges with regard to health care costs and Social Security, Crook maintains that the middle class's quality of life has increased overall with the proliferation of new luxury products including cell phones,

Clive Crook, "The Phantom Menace," *The Atlantic Monthly*, vol. 299, April 2007, pp. 40–41. Reproduced by permission of the author.

video games, microwaves, and iPods. Originally from England, Crook is the senior editor for the Atlantic *and previously served as a consultant to the World Bank and as an official in the British Treasury.*

As you read, consider the following questions:

1. According to Crook, how do modern views of class in the United States differ from those in Great Britain?

2. What income and assets does Crook claim define the middle class in the United States?

3. Crook notes that what percentage of middle-income households in the United States carries no credit card debt?

Englishmen are thought to be preoccupied with social class, and it pains me that I am about to conform (not for the first time) to stereotype. In fact the stereotype is out of date. You might think I'm protesting too much, but the truth is I gave hardly a thought to the issue for years—not until I came to live and work in the supposedly classless United States.

By the time I left England in 2005, class was no longer a very interesting subject. Of course you could still divide the country's people according to sociologically pregnant signifiers such as manners and elocution. You can do that kind of dividing up almost anywhere, including here, since in this sense there is no such thing as a classless society. Politically speaking, however, class in England lost the last of its salience in the 1990s. Today you rarely, if ever, hear a British politician mention the subject.

Class Consciousness in the United States

You could not say the same of the United States, though, could you? In this country, voters and politicians seem to think and talk about little else, at least when it comes to domestic affairs.

The middle class of this country, our historic backbone and our best hope for a strong society in the future, is losing its place at the table. Our workers know this, through painful experience. Our white-collar professionals are beginning to understand it, as their jobs start disappearing also.

That was [Virginia] Senator James Webb, in the Democratic Party's much-praised response to President [George W.] Bush's State of the Union address. He was even more outspoken last year in an article for the *Wall Street Journal*, aptly titled "Class Struggle":

The most important—and unfortunately the least debated—issue in politics today is our society's steady drift toward a class-based system, the likes of which we have not seen since the 19th century.

Webb was wrong to say the issue is not much debated. The middle class and its many burdens and grievances are the organizing idea for almost everything Democrats and Republicans alike have to say about the economy. And it's not just politicians. Commentators are cheering them on. ([CNN commentator and TV host] Lou Dobbs's new book defines this resurgent populist genre in its title: *War on the Middle Class*.)

How strange this American appeal to class interests is, at least to an Old Worlder like me. England used to have, in the European fashion, three classes: posh gentry, professional bourgeoisie, and manual-laboring working class. *Middle class* was a term of disapprobation: To call somebody middle class was to say they were smug and complacent. Clever English progressives, whose political home was the pre-1994 Labour Party, spoke up for the working class; dull Tories, "the Stupid Party," were the traditional representatives of the middle class. Then [former British prime minister] Margaret Thatcher broadened the base, and begat [later prime minister] Tony Blair; and class largely disappeared from the parties' calculations.

Debt as a Means to Advance Economically

Americans are awash in red ink. Consumer indebtedness is soaring, the savings rate is down to zero and people are filing for bankruptcy at record rates. To many observers, these are symptoms of cultural decline, from sturdy thrift to flabby self-gratification—embodied in the current obesity epidemic. . . .

But as the history of debt in America shows, condemnations of extravagance can obscure more than they illuminate. The equation of debt and decline assumes that once upon a time Americans lived within their means and saved for what they bought. This is fantasy: There never was a golden age of thrift. Debt has always played an important role in Americans' lives—not merely as a means of instant gratification but also as a strategy for survival and a tool for economic advance.

Jackson Lears,
"The American Way of Debt,"
New York Times, *June 11, 2006.*

The Clout of the American Middle Class

America's class structure, judging by how often politicians refer to it, has increasing political weight. But the United States appears to lack a working class—the whole point, as [Karl] Marx explained, of having classes in the first place. Instead it has rich people; a politically impotent underclass (for whom nobody speaks up); and a remarkably expansive, proud, and patriotic middle class, which both parties woo. The incomes of Americans identifying themselves as middle class might run from $25,000 (about half of median household earnings) to 20 or 30 times that. In America, it is scarcely exaggerating to say that if you aren't actually poor, and if you have fewer than three homes and do not commute in a limousine or helicopter, you call yourself middle class.

The vast width of this middle, some three-quarters of the population, has long been a great source of economic strength to the country. I am not the first to notice that America has exalted its bourgeois convictions on the importance of work, education, and self-reliance, or that those are the values that give strongest support to enterprise, innovation, and economic growth.

The heft of the country's middle class has been a *political* asset, too. Since the poor don't vote and the rich are too few to mention, the middle class chooses all by itself who runs the country. The electorate is divided, to be sure, but mainly by noneconomic values. The convergence of perceived economic interests means that the political parties in the United States are both far closer to a common economic center than their European counterparts are, and closer to each other than they themselves would like to admit. Policies are presented—and to some extent, at least, must be devised—in such a way as to appeal to this great, broad mass of middle-class Americans. And that is good. If you doubt it, study some European economic history.

The Rich Profit at the Middle Class's Expense

However, when politicians and commentators talk about a "war" on the middle class, that is not so good. Invoking an enemy who is prospering at the expense of most ("decent, hard-working") Americans is [not] conducive to wise policy. It casts the problem as an issue of distribution—a struggle for the spoils. But the prospects of the great mass of Americans, as a matter of arithmetic, cannot be much improved by mere redistribution. There are too few designated losers.

And who could this Other, this segment profiting at the expense of the middle class, be? The poor? That hardly seems likely. So this leaves just the rich—that sliver of chauffeured plutocrats—and foreigners. Designating the rich as the enemy, though, is likely to be counterproductive. Thriving enterprise and magnificent rewards at the top tend to go together. So do a vibrant economy and liberal regimes for international trade and immigration. If you doubt it . . . well, I already said that.

Admittedly, America's plutocrats have been pushing their luck recently. They were already doing fabulously well by any standard, even before the remarkable and somewhat mysterious surge in their pretax incomes that started in the mid-1990s; also before the tax cuts of 2001–2003, so brazenly skewed to their advantage. One wonders whether the administration has actually done the rich any favors, by piling it on that way. Most of the tax cuts (due to expire in any case in 2010) are likely to be reversed by the new Congress. For the good of the broader economy—for the good, that is, of the middle class—the backlash probably ought to stop there, but who knows? If it goes further, the plutocracy will have Bush to thank. Foreign trade and immigration are different cases, and more straightforward. Assaulting those particular enemies (foreign businesses and immigrants) will be instantly self-defeating. Any kind of new restriction is going to hurt the middle class by slowing growth or raising prices.

Exaggerating Middle-Class Problems

Is the American middle class really as beleaguered as it appears to think? That's debatable, at least. The stagnation of real incomes—that much-cited statistic—seems belied by a steadily improving quality of life. Capturing improvements in the range and quality of products, so that meaningful comparisons of incomes can be made over time, is a difficult statistical problem, and the statistics must be taken with a grain of salt. Who really believes that ordinary Americans are barely any better off in material terms than they were in the early 1970s? There were no cell phones back then, no video games; few homes had microwave ovens. There were no iPods, if you can imagine. Life was hard.

The claim that job insecurity has worsened in recent years also seems exaggerated: Overall measures of job tenure and job displacement show no marked change. The idea that the middle class is burdened by unprecedented amounts of debt—that people are having to borrow to make ends meet—is overstated. Most personal debt is mortgage debt, generously subsidized by taxpayers, and backed (for the moment, at least) by highly appreciated holdings of property. Delinquency is rising, especially for "subprime" borrowers (those with weak credit histories), but the proportion of households getting behind in their debts is still very small. You may be surprised to know that more than 40 percent of middle-income households carry no credit-card debt at all.

Redefining the Middle Class

America's middle class does, however, have some tough choices to make. The public retirement-savings system is broken and will require a lot of taxpayers' money—or extra years of work before retirement, or both—to fix. Large parts of the public school system are failing, and the cost of a college education keeps rising faster than incomes. The country's health care system is unsustainable in three ways: Demographic pressures are rapidly making Medicare unaffordable; per-patient costs are rising out of control; and companies are using improving technology (the ability to predict who is going to fall ill with what) to declare uninsurable some of the people who are likely to need health insurance the most. These are real issues. The middle class has grounds for anxiety, all right.

But addressing these challenges is not something that can be done at others' expense. That is the drawback of having a middle class that includes nearly everyone. Clawing back the plutocrats' tax windfall of the past few years is fine, and it will feel good, but it won't come close to paying for solutions to those problems. If America's broad middle class is going to have to pay—and it is—hard questions will follow about how to share the burden between the struggling middle, the comfortable middle, and the luxurious middle. The middle will need to be unpacked a little, and the politics might get messy.

> "Today's up-and-coming American
> middle class has [its] status and secu-
> rity locked up in installment loans."

The Middle Class Is in Debt

Brian Purnell

According to many commentators, the beginning of the twenty-first century saw economic hardship increase for many members of American society. In the viewpoint that follows, Brian Purnell argues that the middle class was hit particularly hard, forcing many to live with ever-increasing debt that they could not hope to repay. Purnell cites numerous causes for the skyrocketing middle-class debt including low wages, rising prices of necessities like food and gas, easy access to credit, and the tendency of students to take out enormous loans to finance their college educations. The author worries that many members of the American middle class will die with this debt unpaid. Purnell is a professor of history at Fordham University in Bronx, New York, and research director of the Bronx African American History Project based there.

Brian Purnell, "The White-Collar Working Class: Has the American Middle Class Gone into Foreclosure?" History News Network, December 22, 2008. Reproduced by permission.

As you read, consider the following questions:

1. According to statistics Purnell cites from the *New York Times*, how many credit cards does the average American home have?

2. What characteristics of class in America does Purnell identify?

3. What factors does the author believe may contribute to the extinction of the middle class in America?

Last year [2007], according to the *New York Times*, the average debt in the United States was $121,650, while the average savings was just shy of $450. You don't need a PhD in Economics or an MBA to know that something is terribly wrong and imbalanced with those figures.

A Shift in the American Job Market

Since the end of World War II, debt has become a way of life in the United States. A host of economic factors contribute to and depend on this scenario. In the aftermath of wartime production booms, the U.S. economy experienced fits and starts in its manufacturing and industrial sectors. Some areas, namely automobile production, remained strong for several decades, but in the face of competitive foreign markets, eventually suffered dramatic losses. Now, Motown [Detroit, MI] looks more like No-town. Abandoned car plants and residential ghost towns having taken the place of what was once considered the "arsenal of democracy," a city that less than sixty years ago was one of the most thriving capitalist centers on earth. Other sectors of the U.S. domestic industrial economy— steel manufacturing, ship and airplane building, textiles and clothing manufacturing—limped along during the twentieth century, but eventually traded U.S. winters for sunnier climates. Such trends boil down to the near total triumph of *laissez-faire* economics: Production became too darn expensive

Average Student Loan Debt by State, 2007

Data show the average debt of graduating seniors at four-year colleges, and percentage of graduates with debt.

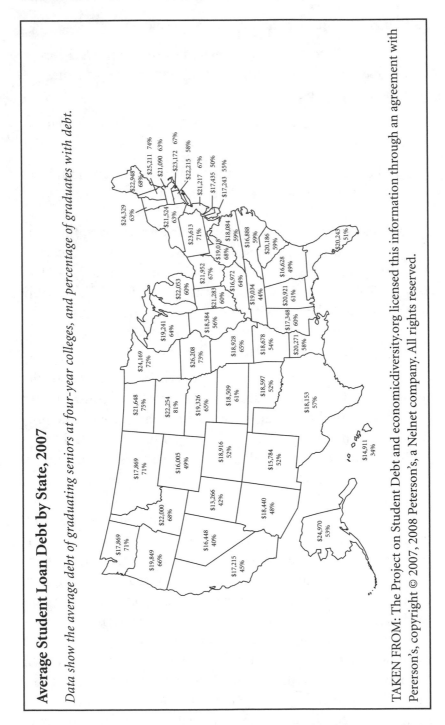

in American cities where workers demanded union protection, medical care, and life insurance; better to move production overseas or south of the border where workers worked on the cheap.

While America was hemorrhaging jobs and eroding its industrial and manufacturing base, the service sector and knowledge-based economy blossomed. The technological explosions of the computer industry birthed Silicon Valley and American cities, such as New York, Chicago, and Los Angeles, along with London and Tokyo, became *the* global nodes of the finance capital and banking industries. Today, 1 in 9 New Yorkers work in jobs that are in someway connected to finance and banking. The service sector dominates the American economy, from those who "wage a living" in restaurant and fast food, fast-coffee jobs to those who "manage risk" for multimillionaires.

Overconsumption and Lack of Exports

At the same time, the United States has become a nation of consumers. We buy the stuff that workers around the globe produce, and we are able to do so at the cheapest prices possible because many of those workers earn next to nothing. In the U.S., the dominance of retail chains such as Wal-Mart, Costco, and K-Mart is due in large part to the massive infusion of cheap goods into one of the largest consuming populations in the world. Another aiding factor is easy access to credit. According to the *Times*, in the twenty-first century, 40% of American households carry credit card debt, up from 6% in 1970, and the average home has a staggering 13 credit cards!

So, Americans don't make anything. As a country, we don't really export much except entertainment, hip hop and pornography. And we import and then buy a lot of cheap clothing, cars, electronic equipment, furniture, and plastic crap, which the rest of the world's workers produce at the lowest wages possible. We don't save, and we are drowning in debt. How does this type of economic imbalance affect class in America?

Obviously it creates both the super-rich and the super-poor. The June 30, 2008, issue of the *Nation* provided a grim portrayal of this new inequality, what some critics are calling a "new gilded age," one that is more grotesque in its wealth imbalance than anything robber baron Americans of an erstwhile era could have dreamed. True, today's American working poor probably live longer, die less from work related injuries than factory workers of an earlier Gilded Age; and there are no children contracting silicosis from working in coal mines. Then again, we have successfully exported much of that misery to other countries. Life at the polar ends of economic inequality is often analyzed and editorialized, but what about life in the middle? Does America even have a middle class anymore, or has the middle class gone into foreclosure?

Defining the New American Middle Class by Debt

So much about class in America is tied up with culture and status, with styles of speech, dress, musical taste, food choice, and comportment, as well as material branding, what label one has on [his or her] clothes or car. Another important characteristic of class in America has to do with access, namely access to housing in particular neighborhoods, access to a particular private or public school, access to social networks that can lead to employment opportunities and economic and social mobility. The middle class in America is extremely amorphous due to the sheer variety of definitions that most people in this country use to explain themselves in relation to other people. An irony of the American middle class is that everyone and anyone could be in it.

At the same time, the middle class may be extinct. As prices of basic necessities, such as food, electricity, and gasoline skyrocket, and monthly bills for housing, utilities, education and consumer debt increase, most Americans are probably one paycheck away from financial distress. Who can save the proverbial "six month" emergency fund when student loans, rent, and gas money whittle away the monthly income of two working adults? Today's up-and-coming American middle class has [its] status and security locked up in installment loans. Only half of all college students in the 1990s carried student loans. Now, that number is over 66%. Some graduate and professional degree recipients will spend 20–30 years repaying their educational debts. Education, which we are told is one's ticket to a better life in this country, has now become one more economic burden, an albatross around one's neck. Add on credit card debt, the incredible competition for jobs, incredibly high rents and subprime mortgage schemes, and what should be the next generation of middle class Americans looks like a population that can barely keep its head above the country's rough financial waters. Wishful thinking says that it's unlikely a rough riptide will pull Americans under and drown them, but tell that to the tens of thousands of people who in the last five years have lost their homes and declared bankruptcy.

The White-Collar Working Class

Class in America as we once understood it is probably now a quaint idea, along with professional baseball players who did it "for the love of the game," and pollution-free environments. Whereas once a "white-collar" job, and the soft hands, starched suits and stable salaries that accompanied it, enabled entry into the American middle class, perhaps (suburban) home-ownership and car ownership, nowadays there is a growing white-collar working class, women and men who attain an advanced education, acquire a "respectable" profession and spend the rest of their lives paying for the pleasure. The white-collar working class is a symptom of over fifty years of erosion in the country's manufacturing industries, expansion of easy access to credit, ballooning in consumption practices, and a reckless culture that has placed almost everything on consignment. We don't make anything and we don't own anything. Many Americans, who once saw the white-collar world as having arrived in a place better than their parents and grandparents, will probably die owing.

For more and more generations, the American white-collar working class, the American dream has been permanently placed on layaway. Maybe the next generation can go to the department store or real estate company or student loan office, pay the balance and take it home, that is, if they can even recognize what it is they are shopping for.

> *"If vast swaths of middle-class families continue to save little for their future, they will either have to work longer than expected or retire with substantially less income in the future."*

The Middle Class Is Not Saving

Christian E. Weller

In June 2005, according to the Bureau of Economic Analysis, the personal savings rate for American families fell to zero percent. Christian E. Weller argues in the following viewpoint that this inability of American families to save has jeopardized not only the lives of these citizens, but also the stability of the country as a whole. Weller points out that these families, mostly middle class, are not overspending, but have too many financial obligations, such as mortgages, health care, and education costs, to put aside money for saving. Additionally, the author worries that assets traditionally thought to hold or increase in value, such as homes, have come to be overvalued recently, making middle-class

Christian E. Weller, "The Middle Class' Lost Future," Center for American Progress, August 26, 2005. Copyright © 2005 Center for American Progress. This material was created by the Center for American Progress, www.americanprogress.org.

families' economic instability even more precarious. Weller is an associate professor of public policy at the University of Massachusetts, Boston, and a senior fellow at the Center for American Progress.

As you read, consider the following questions:

1. What does Weller believe to be the cause of the zero percent savings rate for American families?

2. According to Weller, how would a drop in housing prices impact middle-class families' wealth?

3. Weller states that an increase in American families' savings would impact the country in what way?

The middle class is in an economic bind. The savings rate reached zero percent in June 2005. This is not because many households don't want to save more, but because they often can't. Stagnant wages and rising prices have caused families to borrow record amounts of money to make ends meet. Many families' financial situation is actually worse than it appears on paper because the majority of their wealth is in the housing market, which is likely vastly overvalued. A reasonable correction in the housing market could quickly lower household wealth relative to families' incomes. Without sufficient savings as a safety net for emergencies and as something to rely on in retirement, many more families will continue to struggle not only in their working years, but also well beyond. A reasonable savings policy could address this shortfall by increasing middle-class families' income growth and providing them with adequate tax incentives to save.

Middle Class Spending on Necessities

On August 2 [2005], the Bureau of Economic Analysis reported that the personal savings rate had dropped to zero percent in June 2005. Personal savings are the share of personal income that is not used to pay taxes and that is not spent on consumption, such as food, clothing, cars, health care, and housing, among other things.

Hidden in this calculation is the fact that employers' contributions to pension plans and health insurance are counted as personal income. That is, a zero savings rate means that families not only spent all of their take-home pay, but they also spent the equivalent of what their employers contributed to pension and health insurance plans by borrowing.

It is often contended that the United States is a society of consumers and that people value shopping today more than saving for the future. After all, U.S. personal savings rates tend to be lower than those in other industrialized countries.

However, this assumption only explains a low savings rate, not a declining one. According to this argument, middle-class families should have become increasingly enamored with going to the mall. The reality is that given low levels of wealth for many middle-class families, longer life expectancies, the loss of employers' pension and health insurance plans, rising oil prices, and general middle-class anxieties, middle-class families are limiting their spending to necessary items. Hence, stagnant wages and rising costs for crucial items—health care, college education and housing—have left less in the pockets of middle-class families to put away for their future.

The Impact of Declining Home Values

Another argument states that middle-class families have no need to worry since their inability to put money away today is offset by the fact that whatever assets they own have grown in value. In recent years, household wealth has risen largely because of the rapid appreciation of homes. This appreciation has been so fast that, even though families have typically taken out mortgages faster than their homes have appreciated, the absolute value of their home equity has still climbed. Ignoring for a moment that household wealth is very unequally

Upward Mobility Is Dependent on Credit Cards

For our generation [i.e., American youth who are currently attending or recently graduated from college], credit cards—"yuppie food stamps"—are priceless. . . .

Yuppie food stamps are a shame-free way for millions of supposedly upwardly mobile Americans to keep their heads above water. We may be drowning, but we're still holding out for that yacht. Our schizophrenic popular culture reinforces these illusions—from the rapacious reality shows to the bizarrely secure women of *Friends*: an out-of-work chef, a coffee shop waitress, and a part-time masseuse, all living the good life. We simply aren't willing to accept that even if you play by the rules (get good grades, apply yourself, go to college, work hard) you still might not "make it"—something we've been bred to believe is our inalienable right. And so we continue to bet against the odds on our future selves, laying money down each month.

Heather McGhee,
"The Kids Aren't Alright: Why Middle Class Security Is So Last Generation," February 16, 2005. www.campusprogress.org.

distributed, total wealth grew on average to five times the disposable income of households in early 2005—about the same level of household wealth at the end of the last business cycle in March 2001.

However, most observers agree that the housing market is overvalued. By reasonable calculations, housing prices have risen 20 to 30 percent faster than comparable items, i.e., rents. If housing prices had dropped by 20 to 30 percent, household wealth would have declined to about four and a half times disposable income. Much of what households now show on their balance sheets may turn out to be a mirage. The decline would be worse for many middle-class families who already have little equity in their own homes due to massive new mortgages. After all, while the value of a home declines, the money owed to the bank does not.

Importantly, it doesn't look like families will necessarily start saving more if the values of their homes decline. Despite the massive wealth losses incurred in the stock market crash after 2000, families continued, by and large, to save less than before. This reflects again the fact that many households do not save more because they don't want to, but because they often cannot afford to.

The Importance of Increasing Families' Savings

Without adequate savings, households are moving toward a bleak future. Many households are already struggling financially, leading them to declare bankruptcy in record numbers. Moreover, if vast swaths of middle-class families continue to save little for their future, they will either have to work longer than expected or retire with substantially less income in the future.

Getting America's middle class to save more is in the national interest since it would mean that fewer families would have to endure the hardships of bankruptcy, that people could be more self-reliant in their old age, and that America would have to borrow less money overseas to compensate for the lack of domestic savings.

A reasonable savings policy could accomplish this. The first lesson is that many families do not save more because they don't want to, but because often they simply can't. Promoting policies that would allow families to earn a decent living, such as a higher minimum wage or the right to join a union, would go a long way to help America's middle class save more for its future. Other policies could end the upside-down tax incentives for savings, which give the biggest rewards to high-income people, who often already save enough, and the smallest or no incentives for many middle-class families. Instead, the government could broaden existing matches for lower-income families to save, expand them to middle-class families and make them refundable, so that families too poor to pay income taxes would actually receive benefits from such a policy.

> *"For the first time in human history, the rich work longer hours than the proletariat."*

The Middle Class Has Lost Its Work Ethic

David Brooks

Class in society is often defined in part by the values that individuals within that class hold. David Brooks has observed a shift in these class values in the United States and satirizes this change in the viewpoint that follows. In his view, the middle class is exchanging its work ethic for the supposedly carefree lifestyle of the upper class, while the upper class has conversely become the hardest working class in America. Brooks presents examples of the ways that middle-class workers, who were previously defined by their work-driven mentality, have begun to define themselves by their desire to seek personal improvement, avoid tedious or menial jobs, and maximize their free time to indulge in leisure pursuits. David Brooks is a columnist for the New York Times, *writing op-eds and commentaries on American politics and culture.*

David Brooks, "Bye-Bye Bootstraps," *The New York Times*, August 3, 2006, 21. Copyright © 2006 by The New York Times Company. Reproduced by permission.

As you read, consider the following questions:

1. According to Brooks, what percentage of middle-age men is no longer part of the American work force?

2. What vocations did the two middle-class men Brooks mentions previously hold, and what are they doing now?

3. Brooks believes that middle-class men's definition of dignity has changed in what ways?

In all healthy societies, the middle-class people have wholesome middle-class values while the upper-crust bluebloods lead lives of cosseted leisure interrupted by infidelity, overdoses, and hunting accidents. But in America today we've got this all bollixed up.

Through some screw-up in the moral superstructure, we now have a plutocratic upper class infused with the staid industriousness of Ben Franklin, while we are apparently seeing the emergence of a Wal-Mart leisure class—devil-may-care middle-age slackers who live off home-equity loans and disability payments so they can surf the History Channel and enjoy fantasy football leagues.

Class Role Reversal

For the first time in human history, the rich work longer hours than the proletariat.

Today's super-wealthy no longer go off on four-month grand tours of Europe, play gin-soaked Gatsbyesque croquet tournaments [in the fashion of the wealthy characters in F. Scott Fitzgerald's novel *The Great Gatsby*] or spend hours doing needlepoint while thinking in full paragraphs like the heroines of Jane Austen novels. Instead, their lives are marked by sleep deprivation and conference calls, and their idea of leisure is jetting off to Aspen to hear [Polish-born American political scientist and former national security advisor to then president Jimmy Carter] Zbigniew Brzezinski lead panels titled "Beyond Unipolarity."

Meanwhile, down the income ladder, the percentage of middle-age men who have dropped out of the labor force has doubled over the past 40 years, to over 12 percent. Many of the men have disabilities. Others struggle to find work. But in a recent dinner-party-dominating article, the *Times*'s Louis Uchitelle and David Leonhardt describe two men who are not exactly Horatio Alger wonderboys [the lower-class heroes of Alger's nineteenth-century novels who pulled themselves out of poverty into middle-class lives].

Christopher Priga, 54, earned a six-figure income as an electrical engineer at Xerox but is now shown relaxing at a coffee shop with a book and a smoke while waiting for a job commensurate with his self-esteem. "To be honest, I'm kind of looking for the home run," he said. "There's no point in hitting for base hits."

Alan Beggerow, once a steelworker, now sleeps nine hours a day, reads two or three books a week, writes Amazon reviews, practices the piano and writes Louis L'Amour-style westerns. "I have come to realize that my free time is worth a lot to me," he said.

His wife takes in work as a seamstress and bakes to help support the family, as they eat away at their savings. "The future is always a concern," Beggerow said, "but I no longer allow myself to dwell on it."

Redefining Dignity and Achievement

Many readers no doubt observed that if today's prostate-aged moochers wanted to loaf around all day reading books and tossing off their vacuous opinions into the ether, they should have had the foresight to become newspaper columnists.

Others will note sardonically that the only really vibrant counterculture in the United States today is laziness.

But I try not to judge these gentlemen harshly. What I see is a migration of values. Once upon a time, middle-class men would have defined their dignity by their ability to work hard,

Questioning the American Focus on Work and Success

The men of the mythopoetic men's movement [which began in the 1970s by questioning traditional male roles in American culture] are self-consciously interested in coming together, as men, to explore their inner selves and to grow emotionally and spiritually. They come to the groups in reaction to an outside world that they see as not taking these concerns seriously, a world in which they are expected to perform, to work hard, to succeed, but are not encouraged to feel, to share, and to explore personal growth. . . .

The mythopoetic men consistently criticize what they identify as a core cultural belief in the central importance of work and professional achievement. However, this is not a detached analysis. They speak of how they have unwittingly internalized this belief such that they themselves are some of its most extreme adherents. As such, it is a provocative and subtle criticism that shows a complex conceptualization of ideas of culture and social control. . . .

A majority of the men in the movement are successful. . . . They uniformly identify themselves as having taken on the belief in hard work and material success. However, they have begun to question this lifestyle and these cultural values. For them, it has become "compulsive" and "robotic." Specifically, as seen earlier, they are critically examining the worth of a devotion to work that begins to eclipse other aspects of their life. They wonder if it is "all worth it," if they should "make that my whole life."

Eric Magnuson, "Rejecting the American Dream:
Men Creating Alternative Life Goals,"
Journal of Contemporary Ethnography, *June 2008.*

provide for their family and live as self-reliant members of society. But these fellows, to judge by their quotations, define their dignity the same way the subjects of [Norwegian-American sociologist and economist] Thorstein Veblen's [book critiquing the American economy] *The Theory of the Leisure Class* defined theirs.

They define their dignity by the loftiness of their thinking. They define their dignity not by their achievement, but by their personal enlightenment, their autonomy, by their distance from anything dishonorably menial or compulsory.

In other words, the values that used to prevail among the manorial estates have migrated to parts of mass society while the grinding work ethic of the immigrant prevails in the stratosphere.

Consequences of the Lost Work Ethic

This is terrible. It's a blow first of all to literature. If [British author] P.G. Wodehouse were writing today, [the wealthy character] Bertie Wooster would be at Goldman Sachs and [Wooster's valet] Jeeves would be judging a meth-mouth contest at Sturgis [an annual motorcycle rally in South Dakota]. Anna Karenina [the wealthy title character of Leo Tolstoy's nineteenth-century novel] would be [fashion magazine editor] Miranda Priestly from [Lauren Weisberger's novel] *The Devil Wears Prada*. *The House of Mirth* [an early twentieth-century American novel of manners telling the story of New York socialite Lily Bart] would become *The House of Broadband*.

More important, this reversal is a blow to the natural order of the universe. The only comfort I've had from these disturbing trends is another recent story in the *Times*. Joyce Wadler reported that women in places like the Hamptons are still bedding down with the hired help. R. Couri Hay, the society editor of *Hamptons* magazine, celebrated rich women's tendency to sleep with their home renovators.

"Nobody knows," he said. "The contractor isn't going to tell because the husband is writing the check, the wife isn't going to tell, and you get a better job because she's providing a fringe benefit. Everybody wins."

Thank God somebody is standing up for traditional morality.

> *"New census statistics show that the fastest-growing segment of the uninsured is, in fact, Americans from households with annual incomes of $50,000 or more."*

The Middle Class Is Losing Health Insurance Coverage

Mary Agnes Carey and Rebecca Adams

Mary Agnes Carey and Rebecca Adams report in the following viewpoint on the increasing number of American middle-class families that no longer have health care coverage. Carey and Adams present census statistics showing that these families have lost health insurance at higher rates in recent years than ever before. Furthermore, they state that the employers who previously provided affordable health care plans have either raised the prices on the coverage, making it difficult for these families to continue paying for health benefits, or dropped their health care plans entirely to save on costs. Analysts cited by the authors believe this health care crisis will have a continuing impact on U.S. political elections, until a stable and effective insurance system is established. Carey has covered topics relating to health care for CQ

Mary Agnes Carey and Rebecca Adams, "Middle Class Lack Health Coverage," *CQ Weekly*, vol. 64, September 4, 2006, pp. 2276–2278. Copyright © 2006 by CQ Press, published by CQ Press, a division of Congressional Quarterly Inc. All rights reserved. Reproduced by permission.

Weekly *for over a decade, and Adams is a senior writer for* CQ
Weekly, *focusing on health and environment issues.*

As you read, consider the following questions:

1. According to the census statistics cited by the authors,
   the percentage of middle-class families without health
   care insurance increased to what percentage in 2005?

2. Karen Davis, president of the Commonwealth Fund, is
   cited as saying that employer-sponsored family health
   care coverage costs how much annually?

3. How many of the 1.3 million Americans without health
   care coverage in 2005 had jobs that did not offer health
   care benefits, according to Carey and Adams?

The common perception of an uninsured American has
long been that of a low-wage worker unable to obtain
employer-sponsored health coverage or a jobless person who
must rely on hospital charity care when ill. And for good reason: The vast majority of uninsured citizens have always come
from low-income families.

But the lack of health coverage is becoming a far more
complex problem that cuts through socioeconomic strata.
New census statistics show that the fastest-growing segment of
the uninsured is, in fact, Americans from households with annual incomes of $50,000 or more.

Some experts have predicted that this would happen as
employers cut health care costs and dropped workers from
coverage. But now that it is a documented trend, it is placing
a decidedly middle-class cast on the long-running but as yet
inconclusive debate over how to expand health coverage—and
is prompting an election year [2006] reckoning for some in
Congress. In short, politicians regularly cater to the middle
class, now the newly uninsured.

The Middle-Class Health Care Problem

Census statistics released Aug. 29 [2006] showed that in 2005, 14.1 percent of Americans in households with incomes ranging from $50,000 to $74,999 had no health insurance, compared with 11.8 percent in 2002. This demographic group, which until recently was pretty much immune to pressure from health costs, has become vulnerable to employers' decisions to scale back benefits. Today, having a job brings no guarantee of coverage: The number of full-time workers without any insurance increased to 17.7 percent in 2005 from 16.8 percent in 2002.

Statistics for the population as a whole are just as grim. The percentage of people without insurance last year reached 15.9 percent—or 46.6 million Americans—the highest proportion since 1998, when the rate spiked to 16.3 percent of Americans.

Experts say the trend is likely to continue as employers faced with double-digit premium increases pass on more of the cost of health care to their workers or drop coverage altogether. That is increasing economic anxiety among workers who are being hit with bigger medical bills at the same time they are grappling with higher gas and home heating costs.

"The unaffordability of health care insurance is coming to an employer near you," said Len Nichols, director of the health policy program at the nonpartisan New America Foundation. "The problem is not a lack of jobs per se, but rather that more and more workers are in jobs with wages too low to support rising health insurance premiums."

Nichols said the statistics bear out arguments for overhauling the traditional employer-based system and replacing it with a public-private system that includes government-sponsored insurance pools for those in need.

Despite the recent trends, low-income and working-class Americans continue to make up the largest population of uninsured citizens. More than one-quarter of unemployed

Americans lack any health coverage, with the remainder relying on government assistance, disability benefits, or other forms of aid.

But it is concern over middle-income voters that is resonating in political circles. Proposals addressing the uninsured are already factoring in some political races. In Pennsylvania, Democratic Senate candidate Bob Casey is touting steps to make it easier for small businesses to cover workers. And in California, Republican Governor Arnold Schwarzenegger and Democratic challenger Phil Angelides have floated competing proposals to expand health coverage.

"This problem for the first time is turning into a middle-class phenomenon," said Henry Simmons, president of the National Coalition on Health Care, a nonpartisan group representing employers. "It's in the middle class, and it's people who are employed and who vote."

Finding Health Care Solutions for Middle-Class Workers

There is no government safety net for middle-class workers who lose health coverage, unlike poor Americans, who can turn to the federal-state Medicaid program, or the elderly, who have Medicare.

Some economists have urged expanding these entitlement programs to cover a segment of the working class. However, that doesn't square with a prevailing trend in which virtually every state has curbed Medicaid eligibility or benefits in recent years to control rising expenditures. On the federal level, congressional Republicans, still reeling over hundreds of billions of dollars in new spending associated with the Medicare drug program, are resisting any further coverage expansions.

Instead, conservatives argue, the solution lies in free-market innovations, such as allowing small businesses to band together to purchase health insurance that can bypass state coverage and solvency mandates that apply to health plans offered by bigger employers.

"Some will say that the only thing to do [about the uninsured] is to put everybody on Medicaid, or something like it," House Energy and Commerce Committee Chairman Joe L. Barton, R-Texas, said after the census statistics were released. "Medicaid is a valuable welfare program for the poor who can't afford any sort of health insurance, but I don't think America is going to be happier or healthier with everyone on welfare."

Democrats, meanwhile, are seizing on the new statistics, saying they are evidence that the [George W.] Bush administration and its allies have no empathy for working people and their families. But the Democrats are themselves divided over how to respond, with the options including mandating universal health coverage.

"The numbers confirm that President Bush and the Republican Congress are making a bad health care situation worse," said Rep. Pete Stark of California, ranking Democrat on the House Ways and Means Health Subcommittee. "'Republicans' 'consumer-driven health agenda' is designed to dismantle the employer-based system and put more children and families on their own."

The Impact on Children

A particularly troubling trend borne out by the census figures is the effect that health coverage decisions are having on children.

The Census Bureau reported that the number of children without access to health coverage grew in 2005 for the first time in seven years. Last year [2005], 11.2 percent of children under 18 had no coverage, compared with 10.8 percent the previous year.

The trend is partly because of recent Medicaid coverage decisions such as the discontinuation of some state efforts to enroll poor children in public health programs. States also have been curbing program eligibility. Medicaid typically covers children under the age of 5 who are in families earning 33 percent above the federal poverty level or less. Children ages 6 to 19 can be eligible if their household income equals the poverty limit, which was $16,090 for a family of three in the mainland United States.

The budget savings bill that Bush signed into law this year could prompt more children to go uncovered because it encourages states to charge some poor families more for health coverage.

Children with two working parents are being caught in a different squeeze because their families earn too much for them to qualify for Medicaid or the State Children's Health Insurance Program (SCHIP), which covers children from households immediately above the Medicaid thresholds.

Experts say those families have to pay significant sums for coverage, either through cost sharing in employer-sponsored plans or by purchasing private policies if health insurance cannot be obtained through work. Karen Davis, president of the nonpartisan Commonwealth Fund, said employer-sponsored family coverage now costs about $11,000 annually and that workers typically have to pay one-fourth of the bill. "That can be hard to do with everything else," Davis said. . . .

Employers Not Offering Health Insurance

The census figures showed an unexpectedly high drop-off in employer-sponsored coverage, worrying analysts who predict more corporate belt-tightening in years to come.

Of the 1.3 million Americans who lost coverage in 2005, 960,000 had jobs but no longer received any employer-based health benefits. Last year, 59.5 percent of Americans got their coverage through work, compared with 63.6 percent in 2000.

The decline echoes earlier findings by the Kaiser Family Foundation, which conducts an annual survey of more than 2,000 randomly selected public and private employers. The foundation's 2005 report found that the percentage of firms offering health benefits to their workers had fallen from 69 percent to 60 percent over a five-year period ending in 2005.

Companies that continue to offer coverage are asking employees to shoulder more of the cost increases through higher premiums and larger deductibles and co-payments, or by making new hires wait longer for their health care coverage to become effective.

Political consultants worry that this cost shifting is contributing to negative perceptions about the national economy, a factor that could influence the November election.

"One of the reasons why people do not perceive the economy to be in any better shape . . . is because of the fear of losing health insurance or being bankrupted by health care costs," said Whit Ayres, a Republican pollster. An April report from the Commonwealth Fund found that more than half of uninsured adults reported that they have medical debts or trouble paying bills. Of those, nearly half said they depleted available savings to pay health care costs.

Dan Mendelson, a former Clinton administration aide and the president of the health care advisory group Avalere Health, predicts that sentiment will break in favor of Democrats and those proposals that favor expanding the health care safety net.

"Democrats have a clear issue advantage on the uninsured, and if it can be an issue, it will be," he said. "The trends we're seeing—particularly the loss of employer-sponsored coverage among the middle class—will continue to accelerate, and more people will care about it."

The Imperative to Act

Kathleen Stoll, health policy director at the liberal-leaning advocacy group Families USA, said the rising population of uninsured may rouse Congress to act—something it has been reluctant to do since the Clinton administration's failed universal health coverage proposal was defeated in 1994. "With these numbers increasing more than a million a year . . . there's got to be a point where this starts becoming a national priority," Stoll said.

Some Republicans are uniquely positioned to address the issue. One is Massachusetts Governor Mitt Romney, . . . who this year presided over the creation of a plan that required all residents of his state to buy health insurance and expanded incentives for employers to cover them. Romney lauds the plan as a way of expanding coverage for the uninsured without imposing new taxes or requiring a government takeover of the health care system.

That might work in individual states. But some analysts say momentum for nationwide change will come only if there is a bigger economic imperative.

"This health care problem is now growing so large, so rapidly that it's no longer just a health care problem. It's now created a major, national economic problem . . . a crisis, frankly," said Simmons of the National Coalition on Health Care. "Those rising costs are affecting the economy, deficits at the federal and state level, corporate profitability, jobs, middle-class economic security, and the viability of pension, health and Social Security benefits. It's that big and that bad."

> "The use of the phony concept of in-
> cluding millions of workers in the
> 'middle class' is a major ingredient and
> destroyer of collective thought, action,
> and struggle."

The Middle Class Is an
Illusion to Keep Workers
from Rising Up

Pat Barile

National Board of the Communist Party, USA member Pat Bar-
ile discredits the existence of the middle class in the United
States as a construct of politicians and the elite ruling class—a
fiction that is meant to repress working class collectivism and
uprising. Barile contends in the following viewpoint that no
middle class exists and that only the working and capitalist
classes exist in society. Furthermore, he believes that the middle
class designation, aside from being racist and discriminatory, ob-
scures the repression of workers by the capitalist class.

As you read, consider the following questions:

1. According to Barile, how do Marxist political economists
   define the capitalist and working classes?

Pat Barile, "The 'Middle Class' and the Working Class," *People's Weekly World*, April 23,
2005. Reproduced by permission.

2. Barile does not believe that the middle class is a class in the traditional sense, and instead labels it what?

3. What does Barile establish to be the aim of the capitalist propagandists in defining the middle class by income and not the method by which the income is generated?

What is the middle class and why is it periodically given a status of high exaltation by the ruling class?

To answer the second part of the question first: The ruling class seeks to fool the working class into believing that it has common interests with the ruling class. This is especially aimed at higher-paid workers. Thus, this so-called "middle class" is called upon to act against its own best interests.

Creation of the Artificial Middle Class

The use of the phony concept of including millions of workers in the "middle class" is a major ingredient and destroyer of collective thought, action, and struggle. It is the basic ideology underlying [former president] George W. Bush's "ownership society" and privatization of Social Security.

But it was Harry Truman, a Democrat, who promulgated the "rugged individualism" society. It was Truman who helped split the Congress of Industrial Organizations (CIO). Truman's policies led to the weakening of the cohesiveness of the New Deal coalition forces. He vented his spleen most fiercely against the Left, Progressives, and Communists.

It was Marxist political economists who defined classes in society as stemming from their relationship to the means of production. The capitalist class owns the means of production in all of its varied forms. Workers who work in the factories, mines, mills, and other jobs necessary to the production process are the working class. They have no common class interests with the capitalist class.

There is no class between the working class and capitalist class. The "middle class" is really a stratum. The middle strata

The Difficulty in Defining Class in the United States

In sociology, Nalini Kotamraju has argued that constructing arguments around "class" is extremely difficult in the United States. Terms like "working class" and "middle class" and "upper class" get all muddled quickly. She argues that class divisions in the United States have more to do with lifestyle and social stratification than with income. In other words, all of my anti-capitalist college friends who work in cafés and read [co-founder of communism with Karl Marx, Friedrich] Engels are not working class just because they make $14K [thousand] a year and have no benefits. Class divisions in the United States have more to do with social networks (the real ones, not FB/MS [Facebook and MySpace]), social capital, cultural capital, and attitudes than income. Not surprisingly, other demographics typically discussed in class terms are also a part of this lifestyle division. Social networks are strongly connected to geography, race, and religion; these are also huge factors in lifestyle divisions and thus "class."

I'm not doing justice to her arguments, but it makes sense. My friends who are making $14K in cafés are not of the same class as the immigrant janitor in Oakland just because they share the same income bracket. Their lives are quite different. Unfortunately, with this framing, there aren't really good labels to demarcate the class divisions that do exist.

Danah Boyd,
"Viewing American Class Divisions
Through Facebook and MySpace," Apophenia Blog,
June 24, 2007. www.danah.org.

are self-employed. They create no surplus value. The workers are the only ones who create the wealth. In the struggle for ideas, the ruling class propagates and uses such terms as "middle-class values" which conjure up visions of living in "nice houses in nice communities."

To answer the first question I put: "What is middle class?" Capitalist propagandists say it is someone who has income of, say, for example, $75,000, $100,000, $125,000, no matter how their income is derived. The aim is to cover up and deny the existence of workers as a distinct class.

Phil Murray, [former] president of the CIO, bought into this pro-capitalist, anti-Communist Cold War propaganda in the 1950s. He declared, "There are no classes in the U.S." What did Murray get for speaking boss propaganda? The steel workers had to endure a 116-day strike in 1959.

The Phony Middle Class Is an Impediment to Social Change

The last two presidential election campaigns [2000 and 2004] were rife with expressions of endearment by the candidates on all sides for the "great middle class."

By artificially establishing a dollar-denoted "middle class," proponents of this view leave out, by definition, all those who fall below the given threshold. Among those who are left out you will find, for example, the working poor, the poor, the super-exploited immigrant workers and the bulk of the African American people. The capitalist "middle class" creation is racist and discriminatory to the core, not only in its application at home but also around the world.

During the period of the rise of liberation theology, Pope John Paul II was sharply critical of the transnational/financial oligarchy and industrial powerhouse nations for neglecting the poverty of millions in the Southern Hemisphere, in particular. An expert on the papacy said John Paul II wanted to "elevate the poverty-stricken up to the middle class."

Progressives have a big responsibility to educate and organize among the masses. They can do so confident in the knowledge that the working class will learn to reject capitalism's phony ideological wedge. As Abraham Lincoln said: "You can fool some of the people some of the time but you can't fool all of the people all of the time."

| "The myth of income mobility has always exceeded the reality."

Upward Mobility Is Becoming a Myth in America

Paul Krugman

The American dream of advancing one's status in life through hard work and determination is a central part of American culture and class definitions. Paul Krugman argues in the following viewpoint, however, that this dream of moving up through the classes has become a myth, and rates of upward mobility have become increasingly stagnant since the end of the twentieth century. Krugman places the brunt of the blame for this stagnation on members of the upper class, who he claims have advocated for public policy that helps to stabilize their positions of wealth and limits the number of people who can challenge their dominance. Krugman is a professor of economics at Princeton University and a columnist for the New York Times.

As you read, consider the following questions:

1. According to the estimates of Thomas Piketty and Emmanuel Saez cited by Krugman, how have the incomes of American taxpayers in the four mentioned income levels changed from 1973 to 2000?

2. Krugman states that upward mobility was a reality during what period of American history?

3. What does Krugman believe the wealthiest Americans are doing to ensure that they retain their fortunes and limit the upward mobility of others?

The other day I found myself reading a leftist rag that made outrageous claims about America. It said that we are becoming a society in which the poor tend to stay poor, no matter how hard they work; in which sons are much more likely to inherit the socioeconomic status of their fathers than they were a generation ago.

The name of the leftist rag? *BusinessWeek*, which published an article titled "Waking Up from the American Dream." The article summarizes recent research showing that social mobility in the United States (which was never as high as legend had it) has declined considerably over the past few decades. If you put that research together with other research that shows a drastic increase in income and wealth inequality, you reach an uncomfortable conclusion: America looks more and more like a class-ridden society.

And guess what? Our political leaders are doing everything they can to fortify class inequality, while denouncing anyone who complains—or even points out what is happening—as a practitioner of "class warfare."

A Return to the Gilded Age

Let's talk first about the facts on income distribution. Thirty years ago we were a relatively middle-class nation. It had not always been thus: Gilded Age America [in the late nineteenth century] was a highly unequal society, and it stayed that way through the 1920s. During the 1930s and '40s, however, America experienced what the economic historians Claudia Goldin and Robert Margo have dubbed the Great Compression: a drastic narrowing of income gaps, probably as a result of New Deal policies [implemented by President Franklin D. Roosevelt to provide jobs and economic relief to American citizens during the Great Depression]. And the new economic order persisted for more than a generation: Strong unions; taxes on inherited wealth, corporate profits, and high incomes; close public scrutiny of corporate management—all helped to keep income gaps relatively small. The economy was hardly egalitarian, but a generation ago the gross inequalities of the 1920s seemed very distant.

Now they're back. According to estimates by the economists Thomas Piketty and Emmanuel Saez—confirmed by data from the Congressional Budget Office—between 1973 and 2000 the average real income of the bottom 90 percent of American taxpayers actually fell by 7 percent. Meanwhile, the income of the top 1 percent rose by 148 percent, the income of the top 0.1 percent rose by 343 percent and the income of the top 0.01 percent rose 599 percent. (Those numbers exclude capital gains, so they're not an artifact of the stock-market bubble.) The distribution of income in the United States has gone right back to Gilded Age levels of inequality.

Never mind, say the apologists, who churn out papers with titles like that of a 2001 Heritage Foundation piece, "Income Mobility and the Fallacy of Class-Warfare Arguments." America, they say, isn't a caste society—people with high incomes this year may have low incomes next year and vice versa, and the route to wealth is open to all. That's where those Commies at *BusinessWeek* come in: As they point out (and as economists and sociologists have been pointing out for some time), America actually is more of a caste society than we like to think. And the caste lines have lately become a lot more rigid.

In Defense of the Auto Industry

In today's political lexicon, "Detroit" has become synonymous with failure—a shell of a city inhabited by a shell of a once-mighty industry. It is, in various tellings, the product of individual achievement laid low by collectivism run amok, or of innovation smothered by addled corporate managers and sclerotic labor contracts. Libertarians against unions, environmentalists against gasguzzlers, or car enthusiasts against bad engineering—everybody can find something to loathe.

But, for all of Detroit's mistakes, it is also a victim of something it did right: ensuring a middle-class lifestyle for blue-collar workers. When the carmakers, pushed by unions, agreed to provide workers with a steady level of purchasing power, comprehensive health benefits lasting into retirement, and various forms of workplace rights, they were promising something that all Americans covet. And, while the financial costs and managerial constraints associated with that effort have helped bring domestic carmakers to the edge of collapse, ultimate responsibility for this situation lies beyond Detroit.

In a more enlightened society, after all, government would have made those promises and extended them to all workers, thereby spreading the burden of financing them to all taxpayers. That's how it's done in Europe and in Japan—which, not coincidentally, is the home of Detroit's most successful competitors. But the U.S. government never took that step. So, instead of a public welfare state, we got a private one, administered for only some workers and paid for by their employers. Sooner or later, this arrangement was bound to fail.

Jonathan Cohn, "Auto Destruct,"
New Republic, vol. 239, no. 12, December 31, 2008.

The Reduction of Income Mobility

The myth of income mobility has always exceeded the reality: As a general rule, once they've reached their 30s, people don't move up and down the income ladder very much. Conservatives often cite studies like a 1992 report by [R.] Glenn Hubbard, a Treasury official under the elder [President George H.W.] Bush who later became chief economic adviser to the younger [President George W.] Bush, that purport to show large numbers of Americans moving from low-wage to high-wage jobs during their working lives. But what these studies measure, as the economist Kevin Murphy put it, is mainly "the guy who works in the college bookstore and has a real job by his early 30s." Serious studies that exclude this sort of pseudo-mobility show that inequality in average incomes over long periods isn't much smaller than inequality in annual incomes.

It is true, however, that America was once a place of substantial intergenerational mobility: Sons often did much better than their fathers. A classic 1978 survey found that among adult men whose fathers were in the bottom 25 percent of the population as ranked by social and economic status, 23 percent had made it into the top 25 percent. In other words, during the first thirty years or so after World War II, the American dream of upward mobility was a real experience for many people.

Now for the shocker: The *BusinessWeek* piece cites a new survey of today's adult men, which finds that this number has dropped to only 10 percent. That is, over the past generation upward mobility has fallen drastically. Very few children of the lower class are making their way to even moderate affluence. This goes along with other studies indicating that rags-to-riches stories have become vanishingly rare, and that the correlation between fathers' and sons' incomes has risen in recent decades. In modern America, it seems, you're quite likely to stay in the social and economic class into which you were born.

Using Public Policy to Limit Income Mobility

BusinessWeek attributes this to the "Wal-Martization" of the economy, the proliferation of dead-end, low-wage jobs and the disappearance of jobs that provide entry to the middle class. That's surely part of the explanation. But public policy plays a role—and will, if present trends continue, play an even bigger role in the future.

Put it this way: Suppose that you actually liked a caste society, and you were seeking ways to use your control of the government to further entrench the advantages of the haves against the have-nots. What would you do?

One thing you would definitely do is get rid of the estate tax, so that large fortunes can be passed on to the next generation. More broadly, you would seek to reduce tax rates both on corporate profits and on unearned income such as dividends and capital gains, so that those with large accumulated or inherited wealth could more easily accumulate even more. You'd also try to create tax shelters mainly useful for the rich. And more broadly still, you'd try to reduce tax rates on people with high incomes, shifting the burden to the payroll tax and other revenue sources that bear most heavily on people with lower incomes.

Meanwhile, on the spending side, you'd cut back on health care for the poor, on the quality of public education and on state aid for higher education. This would make it more difficult for people with low incomes to climb out of their difficulties and acquire the education essential to upward mobility in the modern economy.

And just to close off as many routes to upward mobility as possible, you'd do everything possible to break the power of unions, and you'd privatize government functions so that well-paid civil servants could be replaced with poorly paid private employees.

It all sounds sort of familiar, doesn't it?

The End of the American Dream

Where is this taking us? Thomas Piketty, whose work with Saez has transformed our understanding of income distribution, warns that current policies will eventually create "a class of rentiers in the United States, whereby a small group of wealthy but untalented children control vast segments of the U.S. economy and penniless, talented children simply can't compete." If he's right—and I fear that he is—we will end up suffering not only from injustice, but from a vast waste of human potential.

Goodbye, Horatio Alger [a nineteenth century American author whose stories chronicled the rise of American children from impoverished beginnings to lives of wealth and success through hard work]. And goodbye, American dream.

Periodical Bibliography

The following articles have been selected to supplement the diverse views presented in this chapter.

David Brooks	"Whip Inflation Now," *New York Times*, July 10, 2009.
Danny Duncan Collum	"A Culture of Debt," *Sojourners*, May 2008.
CQ Researcher	"Middle-Class Squeeze," March 6, 2009.
Nick Gillespie	"America's No. 1 Endangered Species," *Reason*, April 1, 2007.
Terence P. Jeffrey	"Obama's Class-War Budget vs. Your Income," *Human Events*, March 18, 2009.
Tara Kalwarski	"The American Household: A Nasty Dip in Net Worth," *BusinessWeek*, March 9, 2009.
Maria Kefalas	"Looking for the Lower Middle Class," *City & Community*, March 2007.
Joel Kotkin	"The End of Upward Mobility?" *Newsweek*, January 26, 2009.
Justin Lahart and Kelly Evans	"Trapped in the Middle," *Wall Street Journal*, April 19, 2008.
James Surowiecki	"Going for Broke," *New Yorker*, April 7, 2008.
Peter Wilby	"Inequality Is a Middle-Class Issue," *New Statesman*, June 14, 2007.
Mortimer B. Zuckerman	"Uneasy in the Middle," *U.S. News & World Report*, June 3, 2007.

OPPOSING
VIEWPOINTS®
SERIES

CHAPTER 2

How Do Middle-Class Values Impact Society?

Chapter Preface

Middle-class values are difficult to define. To some, hard work and self-sufficiency might characterize the values necessary to reach and remain within the middle class in America. However, this reformulation of the Puritan or Protestant work ethic—a sixteenth-century Calvinist notion that hard work brought prosperity (a sign of religious salvation)—is certainly not a belief that is exclusive to a particular class. The concept of the American dream is rooted in the drive for prosperity and the sanctity of individualism, and this ethos is supposedly applicable to rich and poor alike. Beyond work, some may tout a high regard for education as a middle-class value in America. Yet again, many lower-class families, as well as upper-class families, believe in the intrinsic value of education, and while a majority may recognize education as a means to a better job, they may not conceive of education as a means of exchanging one value system for another.

Ralph Ellison, the African American writer and social critic, once argued that "more literate values" of middle-class life, of which educated, middle-income blacks were simply ignorant, exist. In Ellison's view, put down in writing in 1975 when sociologists noted that a significant percentage of African Americans were earning middle-class wages for the first time, an understanding of art and high culture were required to gain entrance into the middle class. He chided black leaders for trading intellectual reason for militancy and for leaving black communities without a proper understanding of their place in the "culture and literature of the greater American society." In more recent times, however, one might be hard-pressed to find anyone who shared Ellison's view that this type of "education" was a requisite middle-class value. Some, indeed, might believe Ellison's view to be elitist.

Ellison's argument, however, reveals that middle-class values are often defined by what they are not. Former vice president Dan Quayle once remarked, "If we as a society don't condemn what is wrong, how can we teach our children what is right?" Quayle was discussing at the time the values that he believed America was forsaking. Pinning America's problems in the early 1990s to a legacy of anti-authoritarianism from the 1960s, Quayle said of his generation,

> When we were young, it was fashionable to declare war against traditional values. Indulgence and self-gratification seemed to have no consequences. Many of our generation glamorized casual sex and drug use, evaded responsibility, and trashed authority. Today, the [1960s baby] boomers are middle-aged and middle class. The responsibility of having families has helped many recover traditional values. And, of course, the great majority of those in the middle class survived the turbulent legacy of the '60s and '70s. But many of the poor, with less to fall back on, did not.

In Quayle's opinion, self-indulgence and the social ills that accompany this mind-set were keeping the poor from rising above poverty into the middle class. In effect, Quayle maintained that the poor had to rediscover the right values, and that the government should lead by example. "Our policy must be premised on and must reinforce values such as family, hard work, integrity, personal responsibility," Quayle argued, believing that this course of action would empower the poor so that the lower class might again take part in the American dream.

In the following chapter, various authors examine the notion of middle-class values and what effect these principles have on shaping American society.

> *"The broad middle class that was once the overwhelming majority is being crushed by the lack of desire to work and the overpowering desire to spend."*

Middle-Class Consumerism Is Out of Control

Rodney Smith

In the viewpoint that follows, Rodney Smith argues that the traditional middle-class values of hard work and sacrifice have not been passed on to younger generations, who are instead obsessed with spending money and indulging in pleasures. This loss of values, he argues, is mirrored by the actions of the U.S. government, which also borrows and spends more than it earns. Smith worries that this attitude of ambivalence toward spending and saving has led to the diminishment of the middle class and brought about greater foreign control in the United States in the form of investments in American companies, land, and infrastructure—all of which will have dire consequences for America's future. Smith is a civil engineer who writes commentary from a conservative viewpoint for the online magazine American Chronicle.

Rodney Smith, "The Crushing of the American Middle Class," *American Chronicle*, November 29, 2007. Copyright © 2007 Ultio LLC. Reproduced by permission.

As you read, consider the following questions:

1. How have American values changed from the founding of the country to modern times, according to Smith?

2. What group does Smith believe embraces traditional middle-class values and passes them on to their children, resulting in upward class mobility over multiple generations?

3. What are some of the consequences that Smith foresees as imminent as the middle class shrinks?

My daughter told me that one of her college professors said that the American middle class is fading away. Picture stretching a piece of taffy in your hands. As the two ends you are holding are pulled apart the middle is pulled toward either end, begins thinning, and eventually ceases to exist. Similarly, as the upper economic class and lower economic class are growing further apart, the middle-class families are being pulled either up or down with them. My daughter asked why that would be. I will answer with underlying causes followed by frightening results and implications.

Middle-Class Values Are Lost to Consumerism and Laziness

This is a symptom of traditional middle-class wisdom and values being lost on the next generation. Traditional thought and attitudes in America, aside from any Judeo-Christian influence, was largely stoic. The Europeans and Native Americans they supplanted knew that unless they sacrificed time and pleasure to work long and hard they would starve or freeze to death in the next winter. Discipline was the way of American life except for a small minority of criminals and wealthy heirs through the middle of the 20th century.

As the nation became wealthy, wisdom and discipline were not required to merely survive. Parents found that there was more to life than working and raising children. There were hobbies and other pleasures to pursue. Mass communication provided endless entertainment opportunities, which became time demands. Training their children to be like them (or their grandparents) was not a priority or a necessity. (If anyone has raised children, they know how difficult it is just to feed, clothe and get them to school. Value transfer is another whole layer of love and labor.) The values and wisdom of the middle class were not passed to their children.

Primarily the traditional values of hard work and sacrifice were not universally passed on to the next generations. The values of materialism and pleasure replaced those values. Hard work was replaced by laziness and intolerance for boredom. The values of materialism and pleasure spurred spending money that had to be borrowed. This value shift was not universal and did not necessarily happen in one generation. However, the value shift was significant enough to create an economy based on borrowing and not saving. There are many symptoms that appear in the culture and economy. I will only discuss macroeconomic symptoms and implications.

Pleasure and ease get in the way of work, which can be so inconvenient as Wally [the lazy employee character in the *Dilbert* comic strip] once said. I think most Americans are hard working but there are enough that eschew work as a value to make a difference in the health of the American economy. I have heard of twentysomething children that have never grown up to really work and support themselves. They are still at home: consuming but not producing. I have heard that in some local economies many employers are hiring illegal aliens because they consider the local teenagers are clueless about putting in a day's work.

On top of the value shift, common economic wisdom was not transferred to offspring. A few people prefer to earn interest but many prefer to pay interest. It is common knowledge that the American savings rate disappeared in the late 20th century and there have been economic quarters where aggre-

"Someday, son, all this will be mine."

© Danny Shanahan/Conde Nast Publications/www.cartoonbank.com.

gate personal saving was actually negative. More money was borrowed than saved. The capital to drive the American economy had to come from investors outside of the United States and governments, which also adopted borrowing more.

Government Borrowing and Spending

Our governments borrow money to promote the economy and stay in power. Local, state, and . . . federal governments spend more than they reap in taxes and fees. This boosts the economy, which has become hooked on government spending to keep it on an even keel. The present Congress has overspent trillions of dollars, which has added to our incredulous national debt. The only recent federal Congress that did not spend more than it received was the Newt Gingrich Congress in the mid 1990s. That Congress was castigated by the press for being miserly and Bill Clinton was given credit for the "balanced" budgets. Politically there is no incentive to balance budgets.

Those so-called balanced budgets did not consider that enormous sums of Social Security tax income should have been put into a public savings account but was spent to support federal largesse. Besides the huge debt that the federal government owes to borrowers, there is the looming crisis of commitments to baby boomers that have paid Social Security taxes all their lives that were spent instead of saved.

John Q. Consumer has followed the government's example for spending, savings, and borrowing. Not all but many families have neglected to save for retirement, their children's college, vacations or major purchases or even customary repairs and maintenance. The traditional wisdom of "saving for a rainy day" has been eclipsed by the frenzy to have the latest, the biggest, the best, or the newest of whatever. The endless entertainment media is supported by enthralling advertisements to create needs and spending. There is no money left for saving.

As crime has increased in the cities and even suburbs, families desperately try to buy into "safe" neighbors at greatly inflated home prices. This is a point where the loss of other traditional values has fueled a hopeless housing cost escalation as people try to escape themselves. The present downturn is only temporary.

Taxes have continued to take larger shares of our incomes. Costs have been driven by government regulations, which increase the costs of fuel, utilities, food, and housing. It is hard to imagine any industry that has not incurred increased costs to meet government regulations. These costs are passed to consumers. Again, there is no money left for saving.

The Changing Face of the Middle Class

Therefore the broad middle class that was once the overwhelming majority is being crushed by the lack of desire to work and the overpowering desire to spend. Borrowing replaces savings as the national norm. Interest laden payments consume a greater part of family income. The interest becomes another significant cost that supersedes the ability to save and eventually to consume. Inheritances are lost on debt settlement.

Offspring that do not have family funds to attend college and are too impatient to work through college, start life with a debt burden that approaches the value of a home debt. However, this debt has no underlying equity that increases with inflation. The additional monthly burden supersedes the ability to save and consume. Increasingly the next generation moves downward in an American economy where upward mobility was once the norm. There are fewer families in the middle class.

In contrast those that know how to use interest and temper their spending have had great opportunity to move up the economic ladder. They can create a pool of wealth that their children can drink from. If they also pass the traditional economic values to their children, their children can greatly benefit from launching from their parent's economic shoulders. This is the preferred path chosen by many legal and illegal aliens that hold and pass traditional values to their children. Some move into the middle class. Some pass through it in a couple generations and leave fewer families in the middle class.

The middle class gets thinner and thinner.

The Future Without a Middle Class

There are devastating consequences to the thinning of the middle class. Families that are strapped by payments and materialism continue to free-fall down the economic ladder. They do not have financial options during economic downturns or to personal losses and hardships. Wealth transfer programs are increased to support them. Those on the bottom rung of the middle class have less ability to pay for inflated medical costs.

Taxes are increased or government borrowing is escalated to support them and fuel the consumer-based economy.

Today we find ourselves in a top-heavy unbalanced economic situation where personal debt is so great that it impinges on the consumer economy. I have said for years that our economy is top-heavy with debt and unstable. George W. Bush used the old standby of more federal spending than taxation to keep the fall of the Twin Towers from turning into the fall of the American economy. The housing credit crush is just a slight bobble.

It is common knowledge that foreign investors are buying American companies, American land, and even fundamental American infrastructure such as roads and utilities. We may get upset about foreigners buying up America, but we are not willing to compete with them to even keep our own land. We prefer to buy gadgets from them.

We send corporate profits outside of the United States and enrich people in other nations. In turn they hold not only American assets but the capital and flexibility to buy more and control our employees and increasingly dependent governments.

Future American generations will find they have less clout in the world: economically, politically, militarily, and morally. How can we pressure third world nations to be green or be unionized if we no longer pay top price for their gadgets and trinkets? How can we afford health care or make it more available if the nation's gross national product shrinks? How can we support a high-tech, antiterrorist net in our own homeland?

| "There is no evidence of any 'epidemic' of overspending."

Middle-Class Consumerism Is Not Out of Control

Elizabeth Warren and Amelia Warren Tyagi

In the following viewpoint, Elizabeth Warren and Amelia Warren Tyagi refute the charge that American consumerism is out of control. They argue instead that American families are spending the same or less on frivolities such as brand-name clothing and food, home furnishings and appliances, and cars than families a generation ago. Warren and Tyagi outline the ways in which families are actually saving money when compared to those in the 1970s, and they highlight the benefits of the higher prices they pay for some items, such as cars, that come in the form of increased reliability and safety. While the authors acknowledge that many American families are facing financial hardship, they maintain that rampant consumerism is not the cause of these troubles. In addtion, they assert family spending increased dramatically for large, fixed expenses. Spending on mortgages to buy houses in good school districts increased by 100 percent. Health insurance costs, total transportation costs, child care and total

Elizabeth Warren and Amelia Warren Tyagi, "What's Hurting the Middle Class?" *Boston Review*, vol. 30, September/October 2005, pp. 6–11. Reproduced by permission of the authors.

taxes all increased dramatically. A professor at Harvard Law School, Warren teaches contract law, bankruptcy, and commercial law and serves as chair of the Congressional Oversight Panel, overseeing the U.S. banking bailout issued in response to the 2008–9 financial crisis. Tyagi, Elizabeth Warren's daughter, is a regular commentator on American Public Media's Marketplace, *a radio program discussing current national and international economic and business conditions, and has coauthored several books with her mother including* The Two-Income Trap: Why Middle-Class Parents Are Going Broke.

As you read, consider the following questions:

1. Based on Warren and Tyagi's analysis, how much less are American families spending on clothing today than in the 1970s?

2. According to the authors, how are American families saving on food costs?

3. What are some of the safety features and requirements identified by Warren and Tyagi that have increased the costs of new vehicles?

On April 20, 2005, George W. Bush signed into law a bankruptcy bill that had been pending in Congress for eight years. The bill was written by credit-industry lobbyists, shopped to their friends in Congress, and supported by tens of millions of dollars in lobbying and campaign contributions. It might be dismissed as just one more piece of highly focused special-interest legislation except for the damaging vision of middle-class America that it reinforced: irresponsible people consumed by appetites for goods they don't need, who think little of cost, and who would rather file for bankruptcy than repay their lawful debts. More than just a giveaway to the credit-card companies, the bill was a moral judgment against the bankrupt.

Roots of the Overconsumption Myth

As American families have sunk deeper into debt, they have endured relentless criticism from economists and sociologists, lobbyists and politicians, and the popular media. The accusations are sharp, the assertions are confident and unambiguous, and the tone of condemnation is unmistakable.

The economist Robert Frank claims that America's new "luxury fever" forces middle-class families "to finance their consumption increases largely by reduced savings and increased debt." The documentary filmmaker John de Graaf, the Duke economics professor Thomas Naylor, and the former EPA [Environmental Protection Agency] analyst David Wann write in *Affluenza: The All-Consuming Epidemic*, "It's as if we Americans, despite our intentions, suffer from some kind of Willpower Deficiency Syndrome." The economist Juliet Schor, a frequently cited documenter of consumer irresponsibility, writes that American families are buying "designer clothes, a microwave, restaurant meals, home and automobile air conditioning, and, of course, Michael Jordan's ubiquitous athletic shoes, about which children and adults both display near-obsession." . . .

The overconsumption story gets a big boost from current economic data. First, families have more money to spend. The typical two-income family today earns nearly 75 percent more than their one-income parents earned a generation ago. . . .

But families are not just spending more of what they earn, they are also spending what they have not earned. A generation ago, the typical family owed about five percent of its annual income in consumer debt—non-mortgage debt such as car loans and credit cards. Today such debts add up to more than a third of total annual income. . . .

If families are making more money than ever and are still in financial trouble, surely the critics are right: Americans are overspending, then overborrowing, and then avoiding the consequences by declaring bankruptcy. But the data tell a different story.

For more than a century, the federal government has been collecting information on household spending. It is possible, for example, to find out how much Americans have spent annually on distilled spirits since the 1850s. Here our focus is on changes in spending over a single generation, sorted by spending categories and family size—adjusted for inflation, but not for the increase in family income. If the problem is that today's families are blowing their paychecks on designer clothes and restaurant meals, then the data should show that more is being spent on these frivolous items than ever before.

Clothing Consumerism Is Exaggerated

Start with clothing. The stories of Americans overspending on clothing are familiar: The malls are overflowing, every teenage foot is clad by Adidas or Nike, and designer shops thrive selling nothing but underwear or sunglasses. Even clothing for little children now carries hip brand names, with babies sporting "Gap" and "YSL" on their T-shirts and sleepers.

And yet, when all is added up—including the Tommy sweatshirts and the Ray-Ban sunglasses—a family of four spends, on average, 21 percent *less* on clothing today than in the early 1970s, according to our analysis of data from the Bureau of Labor Statistics.

How can this be? What the finger-waggers have forgotten are the things families no longer spend money on. There's no more rushing off to Stride Rite every three months to buy two new pairs of sensible leather shoes per child (one for church and one for the week), plus a pair of sneakers for play. Today's toddlers often own nothing but a pair of five-dollar tennis shoes from Wal-Mart. Suits, ties, and pantyhose have been replaced by cotton trousers and knit tops, as "business casual" has swept the nation. New fabrics, new technology, and cheap labor have lowered prices. Discounters like Marshalls and Target have popped up across the country, replacing the department stores of a generation ago. The differences add up. In 1973 a family of four would spend, on average, nearly $750 more a year on clothing than such a family would today.

Reduced Food and Furnishing Costs

If Americans are not overspending on clothes, the problem must be food. Designer brands have also hit the grocery shelves, with far more prepared foods, high-end ice creams, and exotic juices. Families even buy bottled water, which would have shocked their grandparents. Besides, who cooks at home anymore? With Mom and Dad both tied up at work, Americans are eating out (or ordering in) more than ever before.

Here the overconsumption camp has it right, but only to a point. The family of four, on average, spends more at restaurants than it used to, but it also spends less at the grocery store—a lot less. Families are saving big bucks by skipping the T-bone steaks, buying their cereal in bulk at Costco, and opting for generic paper towels and canned vegetables. Those savings more than compensate for all that restaurant eating—so much so that today's family of four is actually spending 22 percent less on food overall than its counterpart of a generation ago.

Outfitting the home? The authors of *Affluenza* rail against appliances "that were deemed luxuries as recently as 1970, but are now found in well over half of U.S. homes, and thought of by a majority of Americans as necessities: dishwashers, clothes dryers, central heating and air conditioning, color and cable TV." These gadgets may have captured a new place in Americans' hearts, but they aren't taking much from our wallets. Manufacturing costs are down, and durability is up. When the microwave oven, dishwasher, and clothes dryer are considered together with the refrigerator, washing machine, and stove, families are actually spending 44 percent *less* on major

The Significance of Homeownership

The transition from renter to homeowner represents a significant economic and moral rite of passage. For people at the middle of the income distribution, the goal of homeownership and, once the house is purchased, the house itself are the unquestioned focal points of their lives. Unlike other financial investments, like CDs, savings accounts, or stocks and bonds, purchasing a home is charged with meaning. Becoming a homeowner is the American dream's most conspicuous achievement. Other indicators of status, like a college degree or a job promotion, do not take on a physical form the way a house does. You do not simply use or consume a house; it is where you eat, sleep, search for comfort, care for children, and construct meaningful civic life.

Spend time at any Home Depot and you will know this insight might even be truer today. After all, the consumption surrounding our homes, the endless puttering, the color-coordinated linens and matching stencil borders, and the really big televisions all help regular Americans find a refuge from a world spinning out of control.

Maria Kefalas,
"Looking for the Lower Middle Class,"
City & Community, *March 2007.*

appliances today than they were a generation ago. Furniture may now be leather and super-sized, but its cost has shrunk—by 30 percent in a single generation.

More Reliable and Longer-Lasting Cars

What about cars? At first glance it would seem that the family car might just shatter the case against the overconsumption story. Cars now come jam-packed with features that no one had even dreamed of a generation ago. And cars cost more than ever. In the words of a Toyota salesman quoted in *Affluenza*, "People's expectations are much higher. They want amenities—power steering, power brakes as standard, premium sound systems." At last, a big-ticket item that proves that Americans are indeed indulging in extravagances they can ill afford.

A new car today costs, on average, more than $22,000, compared with less than $16,000 in the late 1970s. The critics might point a triumphant finger, but they would be overlooking an important fact. Cars also last longer than they used to. In the late 1970s, the average age of a car on the road was just five and a half years. Now the average age is more than eight years. Today's families pay more for their new car than their parents did, but they hold onto it longer too. In fact, when we analyzed unpublished data from the Bureau of Labor Statistics, we found that the average amount a family of four spends *per car* (including insurance, maintenance and so forth) is 20 percent *less* than it was a generation ago. For all the griping about those overpriced SUVs [sport utility vehicles], there is little evidence that sunroofs and power windows are sending families to the poorhouse.

The Cost of Safety

The overconsumption camp might still argue that families could have saved by buying cheaper cars. After all, a family doesn't *need* a new SUV with a CD player, at least not in the same way that it needs decent day care or a home in a safe neighborhood. But we pause here to offer a bit of sympathy for the much-maligned buyer of the family car. The car industry's song has changed pitch over the past generation. Glance at an advertisement from any maker of family cars, and there you'll see the new message: safety for sale. The following testimonial is featured on Volvo's Web site: "The driver of the truck lost control of his vehicle and hit me and my wife, who was five months pregnant. . . . There was much talk that 'the Volvo had saved our lives' and I'm convinced it did." Sure, maybe families could do without the twelve-speaker sound systems, but we wouldn't ask them to do without the automatic brake systems, the crash-resistant steel frames, or the dual airbags that they can get only on newer cars.

Safety standards have changed, with a real effect on the family pocketbook—and this is particularly tough for families with more than two kids. Jane Stewart, a stay-at-home mom interviewed by a parenting magazine, described the consequences of having three children under the age of five. According to many experts, the Stewarts should harness those three kids in the back seat—not just with a seat belt, but into a bulky car seat or "booster seat" designed especially for children—until they are at least *eight years old*. Stewart explained, "We have a Grand Cherokee and three car seats in the back. When the baby needs [the next-size car seat], we don't think all three will fit. Then it will be time for a Suburban or a minivan." A generation ago, the Stewarts could have fit their kids into the back seat of any sedan on the market, with room left over for the family dog. Today, even a Jeep Grand Cherokee—a car that weighs 4,000 pounds—is not big enough. The critics may be right that families don't need all those gizmos in their cars, but they should pause to remember that when transporting children, safety and space have become intertwined.

By and large, families have spent prudently on their cars, or at least as prudently as they did a generation ago. And the money they are spending is paying off: The rate of child auto fatalities has declined steadily since the mid-1970s, thanks at least in part to safer cars and better car seats. For all the criticism hurled at car manufacturers (and car buyers), it is important to note that families drive stronger, safer, more durable cars than they used to.

Family Spending Trade-Offs

This is not to say that middle-class families never waste money. A generation ago no one had cable, big-screen televisions were reserved for the very rich, and DVD and TiVo didn't exist. So how much more do families spend today on "home entertainment," premium channels included? They spend 23 percent more—an extra $170 annually. Computers add another $300 to the annual family budget. But even that increase looks a little different in the context of other spending. The extra money spent on cable, electronics, and computers is more than offset by families' savings on major appliances and household furnishings.

In fact, when all the numbers are added up, an increase in one category of spending is generally offset by a decrease in another. On average, a family today spends more on airline travel than it did a generation ago, but less on dry cleaning. More on telephone services, but less on tobacco. More on pets, but less on carpets. All in all, there seems to be about as much frivolous spending today as there was a generation ago.

Whether families are spending more than they should according to some moral notion—consuming too much of the world's resources or buying things they could easily live without—is not the issue at hand. These data give us no clue about the *right* amount of spending. But they give us powerful evidence that excessive consumption is not why families are going broke. There is no evidence of any "epidemic" of overspending—certainly nothing that could explain a 255 percent increase in the foreclosure rate, a 430 percent increase in the bankruptcy rolls, and a 570 percent increase in credit-card debt. A growing number of families are in terrible financial trouble, but despite the accusations, their frivolity is not to blame.

> "No matter how much anecdotal evidence is assembled or how many studies are published indicating that gentrification benefits cities, the myth of gentrification persists."

Gentrification Improves American Cities

Stephen Zacks

Gentrification *is the term used to describe a process in which middle- and upper-class individuals move into a neighborhood populated by low-income individuals, typically renewing buildings in the area—potentially displacing low-income individuals and small businesses. In the viewpoint that follows, Stephen Zacks examines the phenomenon of gentrification in American cities and argues that instead of detracting from the character of the neighborhoods and displacing the previous residents, the process often revitalizes the neighborhoods and the cities by reducing crime and generating income. Zacks describes the recent history of his hometowns, Flint and Detroit, Michigan, and argues that the occurrence of reverse gentrification, whereby affluent citizens leave the city center, has resulted in the near demise of*

Stephen Zacks, "In Praise of Gentrification," *Metropolis Magazine*, December 2005. Copyright © 2005 Bellerophon Publications, Inc. All rights reserved. Reproduced by permission.

the cities and businesses that previously operated there. He believes that gentrification will only benefit the areas and neighborhoods where it takes place. Zacks is the founder of Metropolis, *a magazine examining all elements of contemporary life through design and architecture.*

As you read, consider the following questions:

1. According to Zacks, what misconceptions does the public hold regarding the first two mentioned development projects in New York City?

2. What is the result of failed redevelopment efforts in Flint and Detroit, Michigan, according to the author?

3. What does Zacks believe to be the real reason people oppose development in cities?

A shopping mall opens in a former girdle factory on Bedford Avenue in Williamsburg, Brooklyn, long since colonized by artists and retroactively claimed as their birthright. A cry goes up all over town—the neighborhood is being taken over by corporations! As it turns out, the owners are Hasidic Jews who have been in the neighborhood for generations, and the stores that open in the "mall" are all small businesses—a bookstore, a café, a novelty shop, and a clothing boutique.

No matter: There are other things to whine about. A 20-story hotel is going up on Rivington Street, on Manhattan's Lower East Side, in the last decade transformed from a heroin alley—where shootings were common and cab drivers refused to drop off passengers—to a neighborhood teeming with nightlife and overwhelmed on weekends by the "bridge-and-tunnel" crowd: *suburbanites coming to the city to unload their cash.* Gentrification! But the owner—if anyone bothered to find out—is a longtime resident who invested his own money in daring architecture to create a new local icon.

Affluent Youth Fuel Urban Rejuvenation

Walk around the neighborhood of 14th and U streets in Washington, D.C., on a Saturday night, and you will find it perhaps the liveliest part of the city, at least for those under 25. This is a neighborhood where the riots of 1968 left physical scars that still have not disappeared, and where outsiders were afraid to venture for more than 30 years.

The young newcomers who have rejuvenated 14th and U believe that this recovering slum is the sort of place where they want to spend time and, increasingly, where they want to live. This is the generation that grew up watching *Seinfeld*, *Friends*, and *Sex and the City* [television programs set in New York City], mostly from the comfort of suburban sofas. We have gone from a sitcom world defined by [1950s and 1960s middle-class suburban television programs] *Leave It to Beaver* and *Father Knows Best* to one that offers a whole range of urban experiences and enticements. I do not claim that a handful of TV shows has somehow produced a new urbanist generation, but it is striking how pervasive the pro-city sensibility is within this generation, particularly among its elite. In recent years, teaching undergraduates at the University of Richmond, the majority of them from affluent suburban backgrounds, I made a point of asking where they would prefer to live in 15 years—in a suburb or in a neighborhood close to the center of the city. Few ever voted for suburban life.

Alan Ehrenhalt, "Trading Places,"
New Republic, *vol. 239, August 13, 2008.*

Searching for the Gentrification Displacement Link

It's a never-ending refrain in New York City—a beggar can hardly get a new pair of shoes without a murmur about gentrification. The word was only a rumor to me before I moved to New York from southeast Michigan in 1995, but I was conditioned to hate the phenomenon before I had ever heard the word. As a middle-class lefty with novelistic aspirations surrounded by others of the same mind, it would have required a Herculean questioning of assumed values to have thought otherwise.

And yet reflecting on the almost total lack of economic development in my native towns of Flint and Detroit [Michigan], over the years I began to wonder whether gentrification wasn't a phantom, and an opposition to it a fundamentally reactionary disposition. "Does Gentrification Harm the Poor?"—a study by Duke University assistant professor of public policy and economics Jacob L. Vigdor issued jointly by the Brookings Institution and the University of Pennsylvania's Wharton School in 2002—found it impossible to prove that the poor were being displaced at higher rates than normal in neighborhoods with an influx of middle-class professionals. It was more common for them to improve their economic status. By contrast the systematic movement of capital out of cities—a kind of reverse gentrification—was continuing to have a disastrous effect on places like Flint and Detroit.

"Suburbanization . . . has selectively pulled affluent households out of urban jurisdictions," Vigdor wrote. "In the process cities have become concentrated centers of poverty, joblessness, crime, and other social pathologies. A detached observer of this cycle might conclude that its reversal—the return of affluent households to the central city, associated increases in property values and the government's tax base—would be welcomed by city leaders. In fact the response to such a turnaround, if labeled as 'gentrification,' is quite likely to be negative."

For more than three decades cities such as Flint and Detroit have done everything possible to drive away businesses and encourage the middle class to leave, spurred on by a hypocritical "liberal" mentality that automatically reacts against economic development as if it were an assault on the poor. Inevitably any effort by developers to renovate a significant historic building in Detroit—often for the use of corporations or for upper-middle-class housing—becomes embroiled in endless political disputes that ultimately sink the project. The result in most cases is that once the redevelopment effort fails and attention is drawn to the dilapidated building, political leaders opt for the relatively uncontroversial expedient of demolition. Problem solved.

Lack of Gentrification Causes Abandonment

The failure of socioeconomic studies to link gentrification to displacement suggests that there is actually another reason for opposition to development: nostalgia. Everyone in New York (or Boston or Chicago or San Francisco or even Washington, D.C.) has had the experience of seeing a favorite coffee shop replaced by a Starbucks, a small bookstore outmoded by a Barnes & Noble, a local grocery run out of business by a supermarket chain. As empty storefronts fill up with ever more fashionable boutiques and generic chains, and streets are overrun by crowds of hipsters and yuppies, we're often filled with pangs of regret for a time that once was (usually a year or two earlier). Flint and Detroit should be so unlucky.

On Second Avenue not far from Detroit's Cultural District—where for a time in the early 1990s the gallery hours at the Detroit Institute of Arts were reduced because of lack of funding—there used to be a café called Zoot's in one of those famous Queen Anne-style houses that have mostly been burned down or left to rot throughout the city. In 1994, when I was living in Southfield—a 1950s suburb increasingly abandoned by the white middle class for ever more distant sub-urbs—I would drive 10 miles on the Lodge Freeway for this rare vestige of urban life.

No shops ever opened on the block surrounding Zoot's, and eventually the owner gave up and left. I ran into him several years ago in the East Village at Limbo, a coffee shop on Avenue A that was once, like Zoot's, a lonely urban outpost. Limbo is long gone too, but there are now coffee shops, restaurants, bars, and boutiques on every block of the street. Back in Detroit, just north of the building that used to house Zoot's, a decrepit local dive called the Bronx Bar has been converted into another incomparable urban refuge through the installation of dim Tiffany-style lamps, two jukeboxes, and a pool table. It too will likely disappear before long, not because of gentrification but because of a lack of it.

But no matter how much anecdotal evidence is assembled or how many studies are published indicating that gentrification benefits cities, the myth of gentrification persists. Until well-intentioned people begin to embrace change and recognize that not only is gentrification not bad but it's what allows cities to prosper, every development will confront the same knee-jerk opposition.

A Romanticized View of Pre-Gentrification Brooklyn

Last May the New York city council approved rezoning plans to allow residential high-rises on the Williamsburg and Greenpoint waterfronts [in Brooklyn], previously reserved for industrial uses—such as waste transfer stations—and mostly off-limits to local residents. Planned development includes a 28-acre public park, a walkway stretching along the entire north Brooklyn waterfront, 30- to 40-story apartment towers on the East River, with financial incentives to reserve a third of the units for low- and moderate-income housing. The new zoning should put an end to a four-year-long battle against a power plant proposed in the area, as well as to the pathetic scene witnessed every Fourth of July when locals gather on Kent Street to watch the Macy's fireworks display through barbed-wire fences—with police on hand to prevent trespassing.

Predictably an immediate chorus of groaning was heard around the city. People who had never been to the neighborhood criticized the plan for defacing the waterfront with million-dollar apartments blocking views of the river—which, apart from a small park, is now impossible to see without trespassing. Anyone who has had to sneak through the fence at the end of North 7th Street to hear the current trickle over the rocky shore and get panoramic views of the Manhattan skyline should have ridiculed this nonsense. Instead, they all chimed in. As far as I'm concerned, the waterfront towers can't be built fast enough.

> "Poor renters living in areas 'redis-
> covered' by wealthy and middle-class
> people find themselves in a constant
> struggle to avoid being displaced."

Gentrification Threatens to Displace Low-Income City Residents

Kathe Newman and Elvin Wyly

While recent studies have shown gentrification, the process of upper- and middle-class people moving into previously lower-class areas, to be a positive force with low levels of displacement, Kathe Newman and Elvin Wyly question the reliability of these findings in the following viewpoint. Newman and Wyly argue that displacement of low-income families is still a major concern for residents living in gentrified neighborhoods, and many of the studies on the impact of gentrification fail to report the exact numbers of residents who are forced out. The authors report that in their own studies, methods for measuring displacement were often inaccurate, making the impact of gentrification seem less significant. Further, they state that the residents who are able to remain in their gentrified neighborhoods do so only with the aid

Kathe Newman and Elvin Wyly, "Gentrification and Resistance in New York City," *Shelterforce Online*, vol. 142, July/August 2005. © 2005 National Housing Institute. Reproduced by permission.

of outside assistance. Newman is a professor of urban planning and policy development at Rutgers University; Wyly is a professor of urban geography and chair of the Urban Studies Program at the University of British Columbia.

As you read, consider the following questions:

1. How do Newman and Wyly define gentrification?

2. What limitations do Newman and Wyly identify in the quantitative estimates?

3. According to the data the authors cite from New York University's Furman Center, how many poor renters would be able to remain in gentrifying neighborhoods without rental regulation?

L ast spring [2005], *USA Today* ran a story with the headline "Gentrification: A Boost for Everyone." A little more than a week after the story appeared, it showed up on the Web sites of a variety of organizations and media, including Smart Growth America, the Urban Land Institute [both organizations dealing with land use, growth, and development], *Nation's Building News* [the official publication of the National Association of Home Builders] and *The Real Deal* (a Web site [and online magazine] about New York real estate). Here at last, the headline suggested, was evidence that gentrification could be the rising tide that lifts all boats.

Praise of Gentrification Should Be Reserved

The widespread press coverage of the new wave of displacement studies is part of a broader effort to rescue the word "gentrification." In the 1970s and 1980s, "gentrification" became familiar because it seemed to summarize all of the market failures, polarization, and injustice that shaped life in America's inner-city communities. Developers and public officials learned to defend their actions against the "g" label, because the word served as a powerful rallying cry. But advocates have become much more bold in recent years (the prominent architect Andres Duany even wrote an article titled "Three Cheers for Gentrification" for a conservative magazine), and the new studies certainly provide a boost for anyone who wants to encourage gentrification.

But a far more subtle and ambiguous portrait emerges if one looks beyond the *USA Today* headline and reads the original studies—a national analysis by Lance Freeman, a Columbia University professor; a New York City case by Freeman and Frank Braconi [chief economist of the New York City Comptroller]; and a Boston study by Jacob Vigdor [associate professor of public policy and economics at Duke University]. Based primarily on statistical analyses of housing surveys, these studies were careful to avoid making any claims that gentrification is a "boost" for anyone. But they did challenge the conventional wisdom by demonstrating that disadvantaged renters living in gentrifying neighborhoods have lower rates of mobility than similar renters living in non-gentrifying areas. One interpretation is that the improved public services and other neighborhood conditions brought by gentrification offer incentives for poor renters to find ways to remain in their homes—even in the face of higher rent burdens and other stresses. But this interpretation does not mean that we should ignore or dismiss concerns about displacement.

Defining Gentrification

Much of the debate about gentrification and displacement involves struggles over definition. Although it is often equated with neighborhood improvement, in reality gentrification is a process of class transformation: It is the remaking of working-class space to serve the needs of middle- and upper-class people. Sometimes this does not displace people from their homes, but from their jobs (as when factories are converted to luxury housing); at other times, upscale housing is developed on vacant land. In any case, when an established working-class residential area becomes attractive to investors, developers and middle-class households, the risk of displacement can become quite serious.

The new research made us wonder if poor people remain in gentrifying neighborhoods because of the market or in spite of it. With a grant from the Fannie Mae [Federal National Mortgage Association] Foundation, we set about exploring these questions in New York City. We expected to find evidence that some low-income residents do manage to remain in gentrifying neighborhoods, but we also anticipated that displacement pressures continue. We also paid careful attention to the mix of market forces and public policies that sometimes allow low-income renters to resist displacement.

Difficulties in Measuring Displacement

Displacement is extremely difficult to measure. Yet we can get some sense of the scale of the problem from the 2003 American Housing Survey, which included a question on reasons for moving. The survey showed that in the previous year, about 225,000 renters with incomes below the poverty line had moved at least once and cited cost pressures among their reasons. Of these, 96,000 were directly displaced either by private landlord or government actions.

When we narrow the focus to gentrifying neighborhoods, however, it becomes trickier to measure displacement. By definition, it's hard to find people who have disappeared from the places where we're looking—especially in neighborhoods where gentrification and displacement have been underway for 30 or 40 years. Fortunately, in the case of New York City, it is possible to use multiple methods to measure the links between gentrification and displacement. We drew on a special survey that is unique to New York (the New York City Housing and Vacancy Survey, NYCHVS), and then we undertook in-depth field research and interviews in seven gentrifying neighborhoods (Park Slope, Fort Greene and Williamsburg/ Greenpoint in Brooklyn; the Lower East Side, Chelsea/Clinton, Central Harlem and Morningside Heights in Manhattan). We interviewed a total of 33 residents and community organization staff in these neighborhoods, along with legal services attorneys and city agency staff who monitor housing and homelessness issues.

Many of these neighborhoods experienced some gentrification in the 1970s and 1980s, but respondents explained that the reinvestment that occurred toward the end of the 1990s and continues today is of a scale and pace that is unmatched historically. Gentrification since the late 1990s has transformed New York City, pushing into neighborhoods that had been devastated for decades. During this period, gentrification expanded beyond the neighborhoods with appealing housing stock and excellent transportation access, into those with considerably less desirable housing, challenging transportation connections and few amenities.

The Disappearance of the Displaced

The booming housing market, fed in part by low mortgage interest rates and enormous demand, trickled down to neighborhoods in the form of skyrocketing rents, condominium conversions, new construction and conversions of buildings that were former single-room occupancy hotels. Much of Harlem's outstanding brownstone stock has been transformed during this period from low-cost renter housing to homeownership and high-cost apartments. The average apartment in these buildings now rents for more than $1,700. People from across the city described almost unprecedented pressure from landlords who push tenants out in order to capture higher rents, including tenants who should have some protections under rent regulation.

Within this general picture of neighborhood change, we used the NYCHVS to capture the total number of renters dis-

The High Cost of Raising Children for the Urban Middle Class

Costs, particularly relating to child-raising, are killing the urban middle class. Urban residents generally pay higher taxes and more for utilities, insurance, trash, and sewer than those living elsewhere. Manhattan is by far the most expensive urban area in the United States, with an average cost of living that is more than twice as much as the national average; San Francisco, another city that has seen large-scale middle-class flight ranks second. The Washington, D.C., area, Los Angeles, and Boston also suffer extremely high living costs.

These costs are most onerous on the middle class, particularly those with children. This can be seen in the rapidly declining numbers of students in most urban school districts, including such hyped success stories as Chicago, Seattle, Portland, Washington, and San Francisco. Over the past seven years, for example, Chicago's school system, which was run by new Education Secretary Arne Duncan, has declined by 41,000 students.

America's core cities—including the borough of Manhattan in New York—boast among the lowest percentage of children under 17 in the nation. Although Manhattan had a much discussed "baby boomlet" (the borough's number of toddlers under the age of 4 grew 26 percent between 2000 and 2004), once children over 5 are taken into account, Manhattan's underage population is well under the national average. This indicates there may be a process of exhaustion—both mental and financial—as the costs of raising children drain family resources.

Joel Kotkin,
"The Luxury City vs. the Middle Class,"
American, *May 13, 2009.*

placed during the 1990s. Our analysis revealed that 176,900 renters were displaced between 1989 and 2002. Displacement worsened slightly during the 1990s, reaching nearly 10 percent of all moves, and displaced renters were forced to look farther afield for housing in Queens, the Bronx, and more distant parts of Brooklyn.

But our field research also revealed important limitations in these quantitative estimates. Displaced renters literally disappear from the housing survey if they leave the city. In Fort Greene and Harlem, two communities with large black populations, we learned about the reverse Great Migration to the South. In communities with large immigrant populations, older and even younger immigrants return to their country of origin when they are priced out of their housing. Still others move out of the city to Long Island, New Jersey, and upstate New York. Other displaced renters double up with family or friends or they move into shelters or onto the streets. Some CDCs [community development corporations] and neighborhood groups reported that 2002 was the first year since their organizations were founded in the 1970s that they referred people to homeless shelters. Those who are most vulnerable to displacement, and those who must endure its greatest hardships, are invisible in the dataset. Unfortunately, these are precisely the kinds of crises that residents and organizers described to us.

Assistance Mitigates Some Displacement

Many poor people have managed to stay in gentrifying neighborhoods. Not surprisingly, residents appreciate many of the changes taking place in their neighborhoods—increased safety, less overt drug dealing, better transportation, improved governmental responsiveness and more stores. After all, many of these long-term residents have been working to make just these improvements for decades. But they don't remain merely to appreciate the improvements occurring in their neighborhoods. They remain because these are their communities. Their families, networks, and lives are all there.

Those who remain, by and large, receive some form of private or public assistance. Rent regulation is the most frequently cited form of support. It is followed by a suite of programs that includes public housing, housing vouchers, an exemption from rent increases for senior citizens, project-based Section 8 [housing assistance provided by the U.S. Department of Housing and Urban Development (HUD)] and a state version of the latter. Homeowners of one- to three-family properties are protected by low tax rates for homeowners and a property tax cap.

Data collected by the New York University Furman Center [for Real Estate and Urban Policy] suggest the importance of the rental programs: More than half of all housing units in New York City are either rent regulated or controlled and less than a third are unregulated. Only one out of 15 poor renters living in a gentrifying neighborhood is able to do so in the unregulated rental market.

Other tenants benefit from what is described as the informal housing market in which landlords charge less than market-rate rents, often to tenants they have known for decades. Still other poor people remain in gentrifying neighborhoods by doubling up, living in substandard housing, or paying a high percentage of their income for housing.

The Constant Threat of Gentrification

Poor people appreciate neighborhood improvements as much as anyone else. But few among the poor view gentrification as a benevolent market force that gives them a reason to stay. Poor renters living in areas "rediscovered" by wealthy and middle-class people find themselves in a constant struggle to avoid being displaced.

The unfortunate paradox is that studies showing low mobility rates among the poor are being used to vindicate gentrification and to dismantle precisely those policies that help to cushion its worst impacts. Contracts on federally assisted housing are coming due, forcing tenants to organize every few years to negotiate with landlords and HUD to preserve thousands of units of affordable housing. Thousands of units formerly controlled by state regulation have been lost to vacancy and luxury decontrol, which enable landlords to remove units from the regulated housing stock under certain conditions.

Residents who remain in gentrifying neighborhoods fear that it is just a matter of time until they are displaced. Instead of appreciating the changes wrought by gentrification, these citizens are organizing to create neighborhood norms that value mixed-income communities. They are organizing to press city government to adopt mandatory inclusionary zoning requirements in order to capture some of the benefits from the current building boom. And they are joining national coalitions to press Congress to stop cuts to federal housing programs. For them, the experience of gentrification is not a boost. It is the daily threat of displacement—for themselves, their families and their communities.

| "Middle-class values are exactly what disadvantaged kids need in order to succeed."

Teaching Middle-Class Values Leads to Success

Naomi Schaefer Riley

Naomi Schaefer Riley recounts the positive impact of her mentor relationship through the Big Brothers Big Sisters program in the following viewpoint. Riley contends that much of the success she achieved with her "little sister," Veronica, was based on the transfer of middle-class values—such as an appreciation for education—to the young girl. Further, the author believes that middle-class values should form the basis of mentor programs because these values are exactly what disadvantaged youth lack and what aided the mentors in becoming successful in their own lives. Riley is the deputy editor of the Taste section of the Wall Street Journal.

As you read, consider the following questions:

1. What initial observations does Riley make in her early interactions with Veronica and her family?

Naomi Schaefer Riley, "Big Middle-Class Sister," *City Journal*, vol. 18, August 2008, pp. 10–11. Copyright The Manhattan Institute. Reproduced by permission.

2. What role does Riley believe judgment plays in the lives of successful individuals?

3. According to Riley, what are some of the positive outcomes of her mentorship with Veronica?

Allan Luks, the recently retired executive director of Big Brothers Big Sisters [BBBS, a program designed to help disadvantaged youth by pairing them with older mentors and fostering meaningful relationships] of New York, told me recently that program volunteers should behave like "middle-class surrogate relatives" toward the children they mentor. He quickly apologized for using the term "middle-class": "That's wrong." But it isn't. Middle-class values are exactly what disadvantaged kids need in order to succeed. It's too bad that the people who run mentor programs are often so steeped in bad social theory, nonjudgmentalism, and "cultural sensitivity" that they discourage volunteers from teaching their mentees how to move up in America.

Children Mimic the Adults Around Them

When I signed up to be a mentor with BBBS seven years ago, the initial conversations I had with my mentee, Veronica, didn't bode well. The transcripts would probably read like police interrogation sessions. I would ask her questions about school, family, friends, anything I could think of; she would answer in as few words as possible. And our meetings, which included outings to the beach, the movies, and museums, as well as bicycle riding and even a couple of trips around the park on horseback, were not without their logistical frustrations. Veronica was always late, for instance, often by almost an hour. At first, I chalked it up to her youth. When we were first matched, she was only 11. I would show up at her house at noon on a Saturday and find she was still in her pajamas and had forgotten about our plans.

It quickly became clear, though, that she was only behaving like the adults around her, who had no middle-class values to speak of. The one-bedroom apartment where she lived was chaotic. Her mother, her aunt, her sister, and her two younger cousins were the fixtures, with a parade of her aunt's boyfriends and occasionally her own father added to the mix. Veronica spent money as though she were in the middle class, but she never earned or saved any, so far as I know. That didn't stop her from buying Coach sneakers or a new cell phone every few months.

The biggest obstacle standing between Veronica and a middle-class life was education. My great coup was getting her parents to put her in Catholic school in ninth grade. We filled out the applications together, and despite Veronica's objections—"There are no boys there!"—her mother sent her anyway.

The Value of Judgmentalism

As it happened, the school partnered with another mentoring program, called iMentor, so I became her mentor through that program, too. We e-mailed every week and saw each other every few months. Volunteers in iMentor must be college-educated professionals. But executive director Mike O'Brien says he "would stop short of making a judgment" that there's anything wrong with the mentees' original environment. "I love New York City in all of its complexity," he tells me, noting that, just as many of the mentees hadn't seen the professional world, most of the mentors "had never been to East New York."

The mentors I know never told their charges that there was anything wrong with growing up in East New York—they didn't have to. Mentees saw what these adults had and wanted it for themselves. For a few years, Veronica and I lived on opposite sides of Brooklyn's Prospect Park. "I want to live in your neighborhood," she told me on a visit to Park Slope

Paternalism in Inner-City Schools

By the time youngsters reach high school in the United States, the achievement gap is immense. The average black 12th grader has the reading and writing skills of a typical white 8th grader and the math skills of a typical white 7th grader. The gap between white and Hispanic students is similar. But some remarkable inner-city schools are showing that the achievement gap can be closed if poor minority kids are given the right kind of instruction. . . .

Above all, these schools share a trait largely ignored by education researchers: They are paternalistic institutions. By paternalistic I mean that each of the six schools is a highly prescriptive institution that teaches students not just how to think, but also how to act according to what are commonly termed traditional, middle-class values. These paternalistic schools go beyond teaching values as abstractions: The schools tell students exactly how they are expected to behave, and their behavior is closely monitored, with rewards for compliance and penalties for noncompliance. Unlike the often-forbidding paternalistic institutions of the past, these schools are prescriptive yet warm; teachers and principals, who sometimes serve in loco parentis [in the place of a parent], are both authoritative and caring figures. Teachers laugh with and cajole students, in addition to frequently directing them to stay on task.

David Whitman,
"An Appeal to Authority,"
Education Digest, *vol. 74, March 2009.*

when she was a high school freshman. It was a good opportunity for me to teach her something: "Well, if you go to college and get a good job, you can." I'm sure that I'm not alone in my judgmentalism. The reason young men and women are able to become mentors in the first place is that they made the right "middle-class" choices in their own lives. Of course they're judgmental. Judgment is what got them educations, good jobs, and decent apartments.

When Veronica was about 13, I got a flyer for a BBBS seminar, led by a representative of Planned Parenthood [a reproductive health care organization providing health care to those in need and education about reproductive health care topics], on how to talk to mentees about sex. It started as you might expect: Give them all the information they want about birth control, emphasize the importance of safe sex, tell them where they can get tested for STDs [sexually transmitted diseases], and so on. When the discussion turned to what the appropriate age is to begin having sex, the woman explained: "You should tell your 'little' that they shouldn't have sex until they are in love." I nearly fell out of my chair. Veronica had been in love seven times during the last school year alone.

Veronica and I have never discussed birth control or STDs, but about five years ago, she told me she wanted a baby. I told her that I didn't think that was a good idea yet, and that she should finish high school, go to college, start a career, find the right guy, get married, and *then* have a baby (what my parents refer to as "the right order"). She nodded and said that seemed like a long way off. I assured her that she wouldn't regret waiting.

Recognizing the Victories

When Veronica still hadn't filled out her college applications and hadn't even decided where to apply by January of her senior year, I complained to the people in charge of iMentor. I wanted the program coordinator to make some demands from the school. I wanted the school to make demands from Veronica. I wanted her mother to put her foot down. It was time for ultimatums. Instead, I got more nonjudgmentalism. "I'm sure she'll make some decisions soon," the iMentor folks told me. "And maybe community college is right for her."

This past June, I attended Veronica's high school graduation. Her record wasn't stellar, but she's attending Kingsborough Community College this fall. She has learned something about discipline and hard work. She has had some good teachers. Her classmates have been a good influence overall.

And there's no baby.

| *"Middle-class values' is a code for race;*
it is a euphemism for whiteness."

Teaching Middle-Class Values Is a Euphemism for Teaching Whiteness

Lisa Arrastía

A former high school principal and teacher, Lisa Arrastía writes in the following viewpoint that the commonly accepted and praised practice of instilling middle-class values in minority children living in disadvantaged neighborhoods is really a socially acceptable way of teaching "whiteness." Arrastía dissects the argument of New York Times *columnist David Brooks, who applauds the success of certain charter schools in their effort to teach middle-class values, maintaining that his view is rooted in neoliberal racism, which contends that problem black and minority children are products of their deviant culture and upbringing. This view, she contends, wrongly prescribes middle-class values as a cure-all that strips the children of their culture and highlights their otherness. Arrastía is currently pursuing a PhD in American studies at the University of Minnesota.*

Lisa Arrastía, "'Middle Class Values': A Euphemism for Whiteness in Schools," Social Etymologies Blog, May 10, 2009. Reproduced by permission of the author.

As you read, consider the following questions:

1. How does Arrastía interpret the Harlem Children's Zone executive summary detailing the problems that pervade within Harlem neighborhoods?

2. What differences does Arrastía identify between the eighteenth-century liberal argument and the contemporary neoliberal argument about the problems with African American children?

3. What is Arrastía's final interpretation of Brooks's argument?

On 7 May [2009], the self-identified conservative *New York Times* op-ed columnist David Brooks lauded a New York City charter school for achieving what he considers to be a "miracle": closing the achievement gap between African American students at the school and white students in the city by radically modifying the culture of black kids. Here are some quotations from "The Harlem Miracle" that represent what I consider to be the ideological location from which Brooks sees himself, others, and the discipline of the nation:

> Over the past decade, dozens of charter and independent schools, like Promise Academy [created in partnership with the Harlem Children's Zone, a community-based organization seeking to improve neighborhood conditions through a variety of interrelated programs], have become no excuses schools. The basic theory is that middle-class kids enter adolescence with certain working models in their heads: what I can achieve; how to control impulses; how to work hard. Many kids from poorer, disorganized homes don't have these internalized models. The schools create a disciplined, orderly and demanding counterculture to inculcate middle-class values.
>
> The no excuses schools pay meticulous attention to behavior and attitudes. They teach students how to look at the person who is talking, how to shake hands.

Assessments are rigorous. Standardized tests are woven into the fabric of school life.

The approach works. Ever since welfare reform, we have had success with intrusive government programs that combine paternalistic leadership, sufficient funding and a ferocious commitment to traditional, middle-class values. We may have found a remedy for the achievement gap. Which city is going to take up the challenge? Omaha? Chicago? Yours? . . .

Blaming the Ghettos for the Trespasses of the State

Interestingly, in most of the materials I read from the Harlem Children's Zone (HCZ) Web site, HCZ, like Brooks quoted above, never mentions race, class, politics, or economics. In the case of Brooks, I think he's being cautious. I see Brooks in much the same way the majority of Republicans (and too many U.S. citizens) see people who cross the imaginary U.S. border to do the work U.S. citizens won't do. If I may use this crude analogy for a moment: Brooks is a racism-immigrant, someone who often illegally crosses the border of antiracist propriety and does the work, in writing, that less sophisticated racists can't do.

What we see from both Brooks and HCZ are poor and working-class ghettos—those externally constructed state enclaves of poverty—under what HCZ characterizes as the "gravitational pull of negative forces." The political economy of the neoliberal state is never presented in HCZ's materials nor Brooks's article. Grossly absent are discussions of the social consequence of deindustrialization and deregulated free-market strategies over the last thirty-five years and the dismantling of welfare.

There is no mention of the conditions that have produced U.S. ghettos or the human ingenuity required to live in them. There is no talk of the *communities* beginning to disintegrate when I was a kid in West Harlem during the '70s. I'm talking about those urban spaces where every parent was your momma. In the eyes of HCZ, the fabric of these communities is considered to be "in tatters," yet not for the reasons I have suggested here.

Projects like HCZ are in an obscured and perhaps unconscious collusion with neoclassical philosophies. HCZ's executive summary contends the "things that middle-class communities take for granted—working schools, usable playgrounds, decent housing, support from religious institutions, functioning civic organizations, safe streets—are all but nonexistent." Why are they nonexistent? HCZ claims: "When they do exist, their effectiveness is marginalized by pervasive neighborhood dysfunction." Defective people make defective hoods and even if the "privileges" of middle-classdom existed within these spaces, the defects (the people) wouldn't know how to use, appreciate, or maintain them. HCZ imagines that if the materiality of a neighborhood reflects whiteness, so might its residents.

Addressing the Conditions That Allow Ghettos to Exist

Ironically, an HCZ strategy of which Brooks neglects to make note is HCZ's almost imperceptible admission in their literature of the external forces constructing the conditions of places like Harlem. HCZ implements a social service "pipeline" within a 100-block zone in Harlem.

The HCZ *pipeline*, as it is known, provides free programs for kids from infancy to college, social service and health services, "community-building" programs. These pipeline services underscore the effects on black poor neighborhoods of neoliberal development. By stating what the project feels it needs to provide Harlem in order to enact change it admits that the problems of Harlem are far larger and external to its residents.

The following reader, like many others, thanks Brooks for bringing [president and CEO of HCZ, Geoffrey] Canada's work to readers' attention. But this reader picks up on something missed by Brooks and other commentators. Bill Denham of Berkeley, California, discusses how his son and son's friend were shot while walking down a San Francisco street. Obviously a "drive-by," what we don't hear from this reader is the usual racialized vitriol about the "animals" who murdered his son. Instead, Denham gives insight to conditions that produce the murder of sons and daughters.

> When I received the call from the homicide detective—I can't explain why—my thoughts instantly went to the two young men who had taken these lives—they still lived in their same condition of hopelessness that allowed them to take another life and I felt our overwhelming collective responsibility for fostering such hopelessness in the inner-city neighborhoods of our nation. These children are our children. We allow these conditions to exist.

What I find amazing is to whom Denham either consciously or unconsciously directs his comment: those who believe they are white. Denham speaks directly to social practices that allow us to dodge our social responsibility to *all* kids. When Denham says "our nation" I see a sea of white folks. When he says "our children" I feel that he as a white man (and I am presuming his identity) accounting for the ways in which black and Latino children throughout history and in the present have not been considered a part of a the nation.

Middle-Class Values and Whiteness

What are the "middle-class values" Brooks touts? They are those respected social standards for "American" (code for white) behavior that upon their internalization will produce a child who favors what liberal Americans respect: hard work, a self-governing disposition, and controlled impulses. And, what are the impulses of which Brooks speaks? Does he mean that overwhelming impulse to leave your kid at home alone after school, the ones that make it hard for you to attend a 10:30

A.M. Parent Association meeting at the school? Does he mean that uncontrollable impulse to work day and night shifts so that the child you left home alone can eat, rise up in the morning, and go back to school? "Middle-class values" is a code for race; it is a euphemism for whiteness.

The now deceased sociologist Ruth Frankenberg once generated an eight-point definition of whiteness best adapted in the following way. Whiteness is:

- a place of advantage and privilege intersected by other social categories (gender, class, sexuality, & ability) that may also be a place of advantage or subordination (e.g., white man & black man or white woman and black woman);

- a position, an attitude to or outlook from which to see "selves" and others;

- a complex spectrum of cultural practices that are either seen as "normative" or rational and not racial;

- a culture whose character and identity have been shaped by history (e.g., colonialism).

Importantly, the constructedness of whiteness does not take away from the fact that its presence, its function, its practice, and its process have very real social, political, and economic consequences.

White Values, the Only Worthy Values

Brooks asserts that poor and working-class kids do not have "*internalized* models" of whiteness. In essence he's saying if a kid does not have white values, she has none worthy of respect. The thinking is that if schools provide *real* values, perhaps blackness will be extricated from the child. Arguments like these about behavior are arguments about nature *and* nurture; they are assertions about inherent, innate, or essential qualities while simultaneously being arguments about culture.

And culture is seen as something mutable whereas biology is not. The presumption is that the cultural institution of school has the power to change an innate quality within a "blackened" child that has produced a cultural behavior, or rather has induced the child's culture to behave in deviant ways. The cultural change and the process by which this shift occurs is what Frankenberg called the "conditions and practice of whiteness."

When Brooks lauds HCZ schools for their efforts, he is applauding what he believes to be their attempts to leave behind the irrational, primordial world for a more "disciplined, orderly and demanding counterculture." Hence, he hails their methods for developing good autonomous citizens. Citizens who will behave (*control their impulses*) and *work hard* once they begin work in the service industry for which they are ultimately being trained.

HCZ schools utilize what American studies scholar Maria Saldaña-Portillo characterizes as a developmental approach where the pre-modern savage is moved through various stages of behavioral development until the school arrives at the construction of a model, self-governing (neo)liberal, or rather middle-class citizen "devoid of ethnos." Brooks believes that taking kids through such stages will produce dark bodies who live in opposition to and at variance with difference. . . .

Rescuing a Deviant Culture Using Middle-Class Values

Brooks is, perhaps unintentionally, obfuscating a tension between a traditional, more 18th-century liberal argument and a contemporary, seemingly benign and benevolent neoliberal version. The former says the problems with African American kids are inherent (biologically racial). Neoliberal claims argue that the issues with black kids are not about race, they are about a (deviant) culture in need of rescue and remedy. In fact, HCZ has acquiesced to the social safety gap that neolib-

The Middle-Class Values of Universities

Regardless of what we might say about the benefits of all forms of diversity, . . . types of difference [based in class] are likely to be read, well, differently from distinctions of race, ethnicity, region, or even sexual orientation. That is, of course, if they come to light at all. Students from backgrounds in which education is simply not valued, or in which it is an alien arena, have every reason to hide that fact and to assume that perspectives shaped by those circumstances are illegitimate. The association of college with empowerment, prestige, and upward mobility casts their personal experience as irrelevant. In short, unlike other nonmainstream students, lower-class students are defined as "other" not by those cultural hegemonies of race, gender, and sexuality that the academy prides itself on deconstructing, but by the norms of the academy itself. Embedded in its assumptions about the educational process is a panoply of middle-class ideas and ideals, including the systematic consideration of the un(der)educated, especially in the United States, as a subaltern group. Working-class pride would seem to have no place in academia, which by its very existence encodes class superiority and where students are being prepared explicitly for white-collar jobs.

Janet Galligani Casey,
"Diversity, Discourse, and the Working-Class Student,"
Academe, vol. 91, July/August 2005.

eralism has created. Neoliberalism wants poor and working-class communities to develop private organizations like HCZ that act as single, autonomous individuals—and, in fact, are recognized as such by law. Private entities, both human and organizational, are not dependent, they take care of themselves and teach poor people the same values. Through HCZ's neighborhood programs and schools it has legitimated the state's absence in at least a 100-block zone of Harlem.

And just what are the rescue techniques and the remedies? Long school hours modeled on long work days, academic rigor, proper business attire, and demeanor.

Brooks writes that only "paternalistic leadership ... and a ferocious commitment to traditional, middle-class values" will do the trick. The force of his language distresses me. Do we not meet meat-eating animals who threaten to maim or kill us in the wild with ferocity? Education is not supposed to be a weapon used to tame the wild child, but in this national climate which promotes notions of academic militarism the act of learning, the right to learn is being used violently.

The Reality of Inner-City School Conditions

When I used to facilitate conflict resolution and peer mediation trainings for Children's Creative Response to Conflict [which focuses on helping adults and children find and utilize nonviolent, creative methods of conflict resolution] and Educators for Social Responsibility [which works with educators to create learning environments that are both comfortable and conducive to learning] in public schools throughout NYC [New York City], what I witnessed was a different kind of educational violence than the one taking place in schools, particularly regimented charter and public schools today.

Back then, in the early '90s, under-resourced public schools were the norm for those who worked in and attended them—it was *the way it was spozed to be* for *those* kids in *those* neighborhoods. Going into these schools, I always felt like I was walking into a world cordoned off from the rest of society. Everyone in the buildings knew that no one on the outside really knew what was going on inside.

No one knew about the special education teacher in Bushwick, Brooklyn—way before white folks ever dared to live there. This teacher who would stand in the doorway of her classroom when the kids were coming down the hall toward her room after lunch and bellow: "Okay animals, zoo's open!" No one knew about the cockroaches I saw crawling on the kids' desks *while* the kids were still in them. No one knew how afraid of the rats in their homes and in their school halls children were.

No one knew how afraid eleven-year-old Jean Paul was of the Tonton Macoutes [Haitian paramilitary force who brutally enforced the law of President François Duvalier, who made himself president for life and ruled from 1957 to his death in 1971] who he thought might find his family in Brooklyn and murder them with a machete in their sleep.

No one knew how cold it was inside those schools during the winter where often cardboard that a teacher had found took the place of glass in classroom windows. No one knew that I began bringing extra tissues in my purse to these schools after the day I asked a teacher in the South Bronx to point me toward the bathroom. In a nonplussed manner, the teacher pointed with her thumb in one direction and then reached in her drawer to pull out a roll of toilet paper hung on an old, rusted hanger. "Here," she said, "you'll need this." What was the hanger for, I wondered? When I entered a stall, I was to find some hole, if I was lucky, some hook that remained, and then I was to hang her toilet roll and tear the sheets from it like at home. Perhaps this small and rare feeling of conventional toileting would distract me from the clogged, toilet-paperless, soapless, hand towel-less, hole-in-the-ceiling-pipes-dripping-cage in which I was squatting to "do my business."

No one knew about the schools except the kids, the teachers who dared to come back each day, the schools' staff, other do-gooder agencies trying to plug a dam with their pinky fingers, me, and the politicians in NYC and [Washington] D.C.

It was all too much to hold inside me. I'd ride the train in tears. Sometimes my dad would pick me up and I'd just sit in the passenger seat with no words, just a swelling so thick. And if I couldn't hold the images and the experiences of the schools, what was it, what *is it* in kids that allows them to do so? What plug-in have we installed that makes them able to hold all the horrors we can't?

Institutionalized Violence in the Education System

So, back then, this sort of violence that was standard school fare for poor and working-class immigrant children and children of color born in the United States, was, indeed, not surreptitious. Although it felt like a secret being kept by the city, the state, and the nation, it most certainly was not. This was not a classified story. This was the violent, prevalent narrative of U.S. public education. So normal it wasn't really talked about as much as it is today—not until NCLB [No Child Left Behind, the federal education program enacted in 2002 that placed new standards of achievement on U.S. public schools].

NCLB introduced an additional social, mental, and economic violence. NCLB introduced regulations, discipline, rigor, and not just on the kids but on the entire education system. If schools can't prove that they are whipping their kids into (middle-class) shape, under NCLB poor schools could lose what little they have in terms of funding (as well as their students who are allowed to transfer to "better" schools if their own is failing). Communities have been lambasted for not providing "organized homes" which would "internalize models" of good middle-class values. There seems to be this continuum where at one end we went from thinking that a lack of sufficient funding was the sole problem hurting ghetto schools and at the other, we have NCLB coercing us that the solution lies in a whip and a lot of inculcating the kids with the cultural values and social norms of whiteness.

The Significance of Calling Success a "Miracle"

I want to end here with a brief discussion of the title Brooks chose for his article: "The Harlem *Miracle*" (emphasis mine). I always dissuade my students from using Wikipedia as a source, but in this instance I must break my own rule because the definition it provides of the term "miracle" is very useful here—in addition, the source from which this part of the definition is taken is reliable (British theologian John Polkinghorne). Wikipedia states that the word miracle refers to "any statistically unlikely but beneficial event . . . regarded as 'wonderful' regardless of its likelihood, such as birth." In addition, it notes that a "miracle is a perceptible interruption of the laws of nature, such that can be explained by divine intervention, and is sometimes associated with a miracle-worker."

I think that Brooks has labeled Geoffrey Canada a supernatural interventionist—an angel. Canada has supposedly worked a miracle on those born aberrant. Is it true that only some force beyond the laws of nature could render these subjects docile and the primitive transfigured? This is not the first time that Brooks has subtly essentialized poverty, race, and culture. His "Gangsta in French" was written in response to the 2005 youth revolt in the banlieues [French for outskirts, generally referring to low-income neighborhoods outside of the city center] of France.

In the fall of 2005, after the murder by police of two sub-Saharan, French youth, kids set fire to what I would argue were symbols of state power: schools, school buses, and police cars. In this article, Brooks implies that it was the supposed "poses and worldview" (and transnational, cultural reach) of black American "gangsta rap" that taught poor and working-class French youth of color how to "riot." Side note: France is infamous for its "assimilation" policies. Additionally, at the time of the riots, the unemployment rate in the banlieues was an appalling 30%, which was five percent below the poverty rate for African Americans pre-[Hurricane] Katrina. And, this percentage is only short by about ten percent in terms of the poverty rate HCZ claims that the strategies of its schools combat.

Ultimately, what I hear Brooks, a wonderful mouthpiece for NCLB saying is: Damn you, you poverty 'stricken' colored kids, if you were just more like us, if you'd just been born more like us. If you were more like the liberal universalists who read the articles I write for the *New York Times*. If you were like 'the rest of us,' we wouldn't have to train you to obey our code of behavior and sometimes feel guilty about it. We wouldn't have to sing a school's praises when it, like plantation overseers for the nation-state, teach you kids to sit up straight, look whiteness in the eye, concede defeat, and surrender your souls.

Periodical Bibliography

The following articles have been selected to supplement the diverse views presented in this chapter.

| Tom Bethell | "Our Permanent Revolution," *American Spectator*, March 2007. |

David Brooks — "The Commercial Republic," *New York Times*, March 17, 2009.

Nora Carr — "Courting Middle-Class Parents to Use Public Schools," *Education Digest*, February 2007.

Marshall Goldsmith — "For Young People in the Middle," *Business-Week Online*, August 22, 2007. www.businessweek.com.

Jennifer L. Goloboy — "The Early American Middle Class," *Journal of the Early Republic*, Winter 2005.

Douglas B. Holt — "An Interview with Juliet Schor," *Journal of Consumer Culture*, March 2005.

Richard Lowry and Ramesh Ponnuru — "Twelve Ideas for the Middle Class," *National Review*, February 9, 2009.

David Nather — "Small Steps for Big Problems of the Middle Class," *CQ Weekly*, March 12, 2007.

Robert J. Samuelson — "The End of Entitlement," *Newsweek*, May 26, 2008.

Nick Tingle — "Opinion: The Vexation of Class," *College English*, November 2004.

Ben Weyl — "Trying to Put 'Popular' Back in Populism," *CQ Weekly*, March 16, 2009.

OPPOSING
VIEWPOINTS®
SERIES

CHAPTER 3

What Is the Status of Minorities in America's Middle Class?

Chapter Preface

In early 2008, the Pew Research Center phoned over twenty-four hundred people in the United States and asked them to rank themselves by class. No clear class definitions were given to the people—no income or education levels, for example. More than half of the respondents—53 percent—said they considered themselves part of the middle class. Another 19 percent claimed upper middle–class status, while an equal number (19 percent) said they were lower middle class. Roughly the same percentage of Hispanics, whites, and African Americans identified themselves as middle class.

The racial and ethnic composition of the middle class, however, was not always so diverse. "Our modern image of the middle class comes from the post-World War II era," writes Claire Suddath in *Time* magazine. Her 2009 article describes how the GI Bill made money available to veterans for education and homes, and thus these middle-class cornerstones became available to a large number of mostly white soldiers, sailors, and airmen. By the 1950s, a clear picture of a new American middle class had emerged in the media, and that picture was unvaryingly white. TV shows like *The Adventures of Ozzie and Harriet*, *Father Knows Best*, and dozens of others reflected the image to the nation.

Not until the 1970s did a black middle class begin to emerge. Following on successes achieved by the civil rights movement and changing cultural awareness in the 1960s, the media acknowledged the fact that average Americans were not always Caucasian. "They have become as well heeled, well housed, and well educated as their white counterparts," *Time* wrote of the black middle class in 1974. "Many have just arrived in the middle class, some are barely hanging on, some may lose their grip—but by any reasonable measurement, most appear there to stay." Hispanics and other minorities joined the middle class as well but without much fanfare or fuss.

In the twenty-first century, America's middle class reflects an ethnically diverse country. Social critics warn, however, that the stability of minorities in the middle class cannot be assumed. As early as 1989, *Money* magazine called the black middle class "fragile and shrinking." The 2008 Pew survey "Inside the Middle Class: Bad Times Hit the Good Life" noted that many inequities in income, education, and homeownership exist among the people who defined themselves as middle class. On average, black families earned ten thousand dollars less per year than white families, and Hispanic families earned over seven thousand dollars less than black families. When the Pew survey asked people if they were able to meet their expenses each month, middle-class Hispanic households reported more trouble than other groups.

Just weeks before the Pew Research Center survey came out, an even more troubling report, "Economic (In)Security," identified trends that undermined the financial security of black and Hispanic households. This report from the public policy organization Demos and Brandeis University claimed that three out of four black families and four out of five Hispanic families were in danger of falling out of the middle class to join the ranks of the poor.

Whether the position of minorities in the middle class is as precarious as some surveys suggest is discussed in the following chapter. Some commentators clearly fear that minorities are losing ground gained in previous decades, while others argue that changes in policy and cultural attitudes are all that is needed to increase minority representation in the middle class.

> *"The legacy of the 1990s left enduring and deep-rooted changes in the Hispanic community."*

The Hispanic Middle Class Is Growing

Joel Russell

Joel Russell served as the senior editor of Hispanic Business *magazine and maintains LatinOffice.com, a Web site focused on politics and business in the Latino community. Throughout the 1990s and in the 2000s, Russell observed and reported on trends affecting Hispanic entrepreneurs, executives, and consumers in the United States. In the following viewpoint, he points out that many factors came together in the late 1990s to create a friendly environment for Hispanic-owned businesses, such as loosening trade restrictions, access to financial resources, and especially a growing Hispanic population that was entering the middle class via homeownership, education, and steady employment.*

As you read, consider the following questions:

1. What company did Russell name as the first Hispanic-owned business to post a yearly revenue of $1 billion?

2. Does Russell believe that NAFTA helped Hispanics enter the global marketplace in the 1990s, or does he claim NAFTA excluded Hispanics?

3. According to Russell, how did technology help fuel the boom in Hispanic businesses in the 1990s?

During the second half of the 1990s, the world's largest economy turned in its best performance ever. Between 1996 and 2000, the U.S. gross domestic product grew between 3.7 and 4.5 percent every year. In current dollars, it surged from $7.4 trillion in 1995 to $9.8 trillion in 2000—an increase of 32.4 percent that translated into $2.4 trillion in new wealth.

Never had such a large economy grown so fast for so long. And for the first time, U.S. Hispanics were in a strong position to reap the benefits of the windfall and solidify their already burgeoning socioeconomic gains.

Hispanic Businesses Achieve Milestones in the 1990s

"Hispanic household median income grew 27.3 percent from 1995 to 2001," according to *U.S. Hispanic Consumers in Transition: A Descriptive Guide*. In a two-year burst of wealth-building from 1998 to 2000, aggregate Hispanic net worth rocketed 31.2 percent to $512 billion, concludes the report, available at www.hispanicbusiness.com/research.

For *Hispanic Business* magazine, the decade represented fulfillment of a promise. For years the magazine had been uncovering and revealing data and trends that projected the emergence of a Hispanic middle class. Suddenly, all of the numbers proved it. In 1999, 48.4 percent of Hispanic families owned their own homes. Voter registration (34.9 percent of voting-age Hispanics) and turnout (27.1 percent) were at record levels. By the December 1999 issue of the magazine, total Hispanic purchasing power was estimated at $272.7 billion. . . .

In 1990, the *Hispanic Business 500* reported cumulative revenues of $8.3 billion; by 1999, that figure had more than doubled to $17.4 billion. The largest company on the list in 1999, Miami-based MasTec Inc., reached another milestone by becoming the first Hispanic-owned company to post annual revenues of $1 billion. "MasTec is simply proof of what many already understand—that the Hispanic community has a vast reservoir of potential that, if given the chance, can reach unprecedented heights," said Áida Álvarez, administrator of the Small Business Administration. George Herrera, CEO [chief executive officer] of the U.S. Hispanic Chamber of Commerce, called MasTec's achievement "a clear indication that the Hispanic business community has entered the economic mainstream."

MasTec wasn't the only company showing success. Another Miami-based company, the Vincam Group, had actually looked certain to beat MasTec to the $1 billion mark. But before the company hit that threshold, CEO Carlos Saladrigas sold it to publicly traded ADP [Automatic Data Processing, Inc.]. MasTec eventually won the race, in large part by going public itself and using the proceeds to buy smaller competitors. "Our listing on the New York Stock Exchange has had a significant impact on our business," CEO Jorge Mas told *Hispanic Business* in June 1999. "Access to capital has been instrumental in helping us . . . acquire companies that fit into our plan and fund overall growth."

Access to Capital and Changing Demographics Fuel Prosperity

In the 1990s, it was this issue of access to capital that would emerge as a major issue in U.S. Hispanic business development. In the Hispanic media market, consolidation created large conglomerates with vast financial resources. During this decade, Univision, Telemundo, Hispanic Broadcasting Corp., and Radio Unica all held initial public offerings. In late 1999,

Hispanic Women Entrepreneurs Are on the Rise

Hispanic women entrepreneurs lead the Hispanic business growth, starting businesses at a rate six times the national average, according to the U.S. Hispanic Chamber of Commerce.

"Hispanic women are supporting each other," said Lillian Kim, who in 2000 opened Brownsville-based Key Mortgage Co., which has offices in Harlingen and McAllen. She also is chairwoman of Cameron Works, a Cameron County workforce development agency.

Hispanic women entrepreneurs come from a culture that values a tight-knit family unit, she said, and when one Hispanic woman starts a business, it makes entrepreneurship easier for another Hispanic woman as the women can support each other.

Matt Whittaker,
"Hispanic Business Ventures Booming,"
Valley Morning Star *(Harlingen, TX), March 26, 2006.*

Spanish Broadcasting System staged the second-most successful IPO [initial public stock offering] in the history of radio, selling $501 million in stock.

But it was demographic trends during this decade that underpinned the success of Hispanic media and the broader Hispanic market. "The Hispanic population grew 57.9 percent in the 1990s," according to *Hispanic Consumers in Transition*. A significant portion of this population growth came from high Hispanic birth rates in the United States, bolstered by strong, steady immigration. By the end of the decade, a population bubble of young Hispanics had entered the U.S. school system as well as the entry-level job market. In response, *Hispanic*

Business launched *SuperOnda*, a new magazine specifically tailored to the youth market and its ambitions for economic progress.

Besides national prosperity, two other trends pulled U.S. Hispanics toward the center of the global economy. First came a loosening of trade restrictions with Latin America. In 1994, the United States, Mexico, and Canada joined in the North American Free Trade Agreement (NAFTA). By 1999, two-way U.S.-Mexico trade had nearly doubled to $196.6 billion. Meanwhile, democratic governments in Argentina, Chile, Brazil, Venezuela, and Colombia were testing the merits of capitalism. Privatization and growth opportunities for multinational corporations encouraged a wave of foreign investment into the region. To monitor and chronicle U.S. Hispanics' penetration of foreign markets, *Hispanic Business* began publishing an annual directory in 1995 of the Top 50 Exporters.

Technology provided the other impetus toward global thinking. The Internet exploded on the scene between 1996 and 1998, capturing the imagination of CEOs and consumers alike. The cross-border reach of the Internet inspired the idea of pan-regional Web sites accessible to all Spanish speakers. Despite worries about a potentially slower Hispanic adoption of technology (the so-called Digital Divide), companies such as Quepasa.com, Latino.com, StarMedia, and ElSitio.com attempted to create Hispanic portals to the Web. . . .

Looking Ahead to Greater Growth

Like the boom-and-bust cycles of previous generations, however, the dot-com euphoria peaked in early 2000, and the resulting slowdown spread to telecommunications, media, advertising, and hardware manufacturing. Still, the legacy of the 1990s left enduring and deep-rooted changes in the Hispanic community. Sectors such as finance, travel, and specialty retailing have moved to the Internet. E-mail has become the standard communication medium in corporate America. For the Hispanic middle class, the sense of economic advancement achieved in the 1990s would position them to exert even greater influence in the U.S. economy and culture in the 21st century. And it would give them the strength and stability to weather the global economic challenges that would lie ahead.

"As the Hispanic population grows, so should the number of Hispanics who are middle class. But this will not happen without the support of effective public policy, especially given today's disparities."

Government Policy Reform Is Necessary for the Hispanic Middle Class to Grow

Jennifer Wheary

Jennifer Wheary is a senior fellow with Demos, a public policy research organization, where she studies the changing demographics and factors that affect America's middle class. In the viewpoint that follows, Wheary argues that government policies founded in the mid-twentieth century helped create educational and economic opportunities that allowed a middle class to thrive at that time. Now, she maintains, such policies need to be established to help the fast-growing Hispanic population in the United States. Only with government assistance in homeownership, higher education, and increased income can predominantly poor Hispanics join the middle class, Wheary claims.

Jennifer Wheary, "The Future Hispanic Middle Class," *Around the Kitchen Table*, vol. 5, April 2005, pp. 8–9. Reproduced by permission.

As you read, consider the following questions:

1. What policies does Wheary mention that helped many Americans get a college education in the post-World War II era?

2. According to Wheary, how does the number of Hispanic college graduates compare to white college graduates?

3. Which ethnic group does Wheary say is more likely to own stocks and mutual funds?

In the years following WWII [World War II], public policies built an infrastructure of opportunity that lifted millions of (mostly white) Americans into the middle class. These policies supported the development of a middle class by focusing on education, homeownership, income growth, and wealth building. With demographics projecting an increasingly Hispanic America, it's past time to reinvest in policies that will build a diverse future middle class.

Policies focused on these areas still have an important role to play in building tomorrow's middle class. But, if this role is to be an effective one, we need to be aware of the ways in which past efforts have fallen short. In the post-war years, government programs made higher education and economic opportunity available to a larger group of people than ever before.

The [1944] GI [a member of the U.S. armed forces] Bill made college possible for many veterans. The Higher Education Act of 1965 provided need-based aid for low-income students and helped close both class and race gaps in college enrollment. Federal housing policy and government-backed programs helped would-be home buyers with down payments and enabled more people to get mortgages. The home mortgage interest deduction offered needed support to families pursuing the American dream. Public investment in roads, federal support for cheap gasoline, and other government-backed groundwork laid the foundation for new suburban housing. Industry reforms targeted discriminatory lending practices. Labor and economic policies raised the minimum wage to its peak value in 1968, bolstered the economy, ensured a tight employment market, facilitated union organizing, and helped grow incomes and build wealth.

Hispanics' Gains Don't Keep Them Even with Whites

Hispanics are the fastest growing ethnic group in the country. Over the next five decades, the number of Hispanics in the United States is estimated to grow 188 percent, a rate twenty-six times greater than that of whites. By 2050, one in four Americans will be Hispanic. By the numbers, Hispanics should have a significant place in the future middle class. But this place is far from secure. In 2005, Hispanics are disproportionately large as a percentage of the poorest Americans, and disproportionately small as a percentage of the most well-off.

Higher education, homeownership, income, and wealth are keys to building a middle class. Emphasize these areas, as happened in America's post-WWII policy experiment, and opportunity grows. Deemphasize them, as has happened in recent years, and opportunity stagnates. Much more work is needed to close the gaps that currently exist between Hispanics and whites. This work is urgent if we want to ensure that today's gaps do not become tomorrow's chasms.

Between 1974–2003, the number of Hispanic college graduates more than doubled. Today, a little more than 10 percent of Hispanics hold a four-year college degree. But for whites, that number is about one in three. Even with the dramatic increase over the last three decades in the percentage of Hispanics graduating from college, Hispanics are still 62 percent less likely than whites to hold four-year degrees.

Median Personal Earnings, by Race and Ethnicity, 2007	
	Median earnings ($)
Hispanic	21,048
Native born	23,274
Foreign born	20,238
White alone, not Hispanic	30,357
Black alone, not Hispanic	24,286
Asian alone, not Hispanic	32,786
Other, not Hispanic	22,262
All	28,333

TAKEN FROM: Pew Hispanic Center, "Statistical Portrait of Hispanics in the United States, 2007," March 5, 2009.

In Economic Matters, Hispanics Make Slow Progress

Hispanic homeownership rates grew 9 percent over the last three decades, and today about one out of two Hispanics is a homeowner. In comparison, more than three-quarters of whites own their homes. In fact, whites are nearly two-thirds more likely than Hispanics to be homeowners.

Middle incomes among Hispanics have grown over the last three decades. Incomes among the middle 40 percent of Hispanic earners are up 12 percent. The number of Hispanic households earning between $35,000–$74,999 (in constant dollars) has grown 7 percent. Yet the earnings of Hispanics and whites are still worlds apart. For every dollar in income earned by a white household, a Hispanic household earns just 69 cents.

Wealth is an essential component of social mobility, one that enables opportunity across generations. Despite its importance in enabling future opportunity, wealth remains an area of inconsistent growth and extreme disparity between white and Hispanic households. Over the last two decades, the number of Hispanic households owning stocks and mutual funds has grown an encouraging 23 percent. But in the same time frame, the number of Hispanic households holding interest-bearing assets at financial institutions actually declined by 8 percent. Even with past growth, Hispanic households are still two and a half times less likely than white households to hold stock and mutual funds. Overall, Hispanics own less than 13 cents in wealth for every dollar in wealth held by white households.

In an era where the Hispanic population is growing at a rate that is twenty-six times faster than the white population, disparities in areas that secure entry into the middle class have important implications for the future of the nation. As the Hispanic population grows, so should the number of Hispanics who are middle class. But this will not happen without the support of effective public policy, especially given today's disparities. Promoting access to higher education, encouraging homeownership, growing incomes, and helping to build wealth are not new goals. They are in fact areas where we can claim past, albeit incomplete, success. We need to learn from that success and aim to complete it by focusing our efforts on the next generation of Americans.

"The black middle class continues to grow when examining black households with householders in the 25- to 54- and 25- to 44-year-old ranges, and that the Love Jones Cohort could be the leading cause of this growth."

The Demographics of Middle-Class Blacks Are Changing

Kris Marsh et al.

Kris Marsh is a professor of sociology and the director of the Carolina Population Center at the University of North Carolina at Chapel Hill. With other researchers, she examined statistics on black households in the United States, and in the following viewpoint, she contends that single adults without children make up a large portion of the black middle class. Marsh and her colleagues acknowledge that married adults and families are holding their own in the middle class, but the research indicates that the overlooked demographic of single adults is largely responsible for the growth of the black middle class.

Kris Marsh, William A. Darity Jr., Philip N. Cohen, Lynne M. Casper and Danielle Salters, "The Emerging Black Middle Class: Single and Living Alone," *Social Forces*, vol. 86, December 2007, pp. 735–762. Copyright © 2007 by the University of North Carolina Press. Used by permission.

As you read, consider the following questions:

1. What age group do Marsh and the other authors refer to as the "Love Jones Cohort"?

2. What happened to the percent of SALA black households between 1980 and 2000, as Marsh and her colleagues relate?

3. According to the research, who has a greater chance of being in the black middle class, married couples with children or married couples without children?

Over the past three decades in the United States, the age of marriage has risen, divorce rates have remained relatively stable, cohabitation has soared, nonmarital childbearing has become more prevalent, marrying and having children have become less common, and more women, especially mothers, are in the labor force. With the exception of the trend toward not having children, these trends have been dramatically evident among blacks. The retreat from marriage, in particular, has been more pronounced for blacks than for any other racial group.

These changes in family patterns invite questions about the demographics of the black middle class. Research on the black middle class has focused predominantly on married-couple families with children, reflecting a conception of the black middle class as principally composed of this family type. If that conception is correct, then declining rates of marriage and childrearing would imply a decline in the presence and vitality of the black middle class. Indeed, this is the implication that researchers typically draw from the decline in black marriage rates. However, an alternative view suggests that the decline in marriage and childrearing is producing a shift in the types of households comprising the black middle class away from married couples with children and toward singles living alone. . . .

The Love Jones Cohort

Numerous studies reinforce the generalization that married-couple family households with children tend to be middle class and that single and/or divorced households—the U.S. Census Bureau category that includes single-parent households—tend to be poor. However, popular media, such as TV and film, may be emulating reality by depicting a new kind of middle-class black: young, never-married, urban professionals living alone. Films focusing on this new demographic profile include *Love Jones* (1997), about a young black male poet in Chicago who dates a talented female photographer, and *The Brothers* (2001), in which four black male friends begin to question their intimate relationships when one of them announces his impending marriage. To this list could be added the sitcom *Girlfriends* (TV series, 2000-[2008]), about four young black women managing their professional and personal lives. These media depictions invite a reexamination of demographic shifts in the black middle class as a result of changing family patterns. Do these popular representations of a new black middle class reflect an actual demographic change?

Taking a cue from the acronyms that have been offered by the U.S. Census Bureau to describe different family configurations—such as DEWKs (dual earners with kids) or DINKs (dual income, no kids)—this study refers to households comprised of one person who is never-married (hereafter referred to as single) and living alone as SALA (single and living alone). Borrowing the title of one of the popular films mentioned above, we dub these black middle-class SALAs the "Love Jones Cohort." The operational characteristics used to identify the Love Jones Cohort are the following: blacks, ages 25 through 44, who live alone, are single (never married), hold high-wage occupations, have advanced degrees, maintain household incomes above average and own their own homes. . . .

Defining Households

The U.S. Census Bureau divides households into two categories: family and nonfamily. A family household is one in which members are related to the householder through blood, marriage or adoption. Family households are then subdivided into married-couple families and other families. A *married-couple family household* has both spouses present in the same household. *Other-family households* consist of an unmarried householder, with no spouse present, and at least one family member related through blood, marriage or adoption (e.g., children). Members of *nonfamily households* are not related through blood or marriage, and children are not present. SALA is one type of nonfamily household—one-person households in which the householder is single (never married) and living alone. Other examples of nonfamily households include two or more unrelated and unmarried persons sharing a living unit as roommates or cohabitors living without children.

Researchers who equate married-couple families with the black middle class are not considering the possibility that the rise in the number of nonfamily households in the black population represents a significant segment of the black middle class. . . .

If we are correct about the growth of the Love Jones Cohort, it would appear that this group has a different set of strategies for stabilizing its class position. Contrary to the prevailing assumption in the literature, this cohort stabilizes its position *by not marrying and continuing to live alone*. Indeed, when the complications of per person income are taken into account, SALAs may have certain advantages in maintaining middle-class status over married couples. . . .

Defining the Black Middle Class

Scholars have struggled for decades to decide who among the black population should be considered middle class. Quantitative definitions of the black middle class generally rely on four variables, used either in combination with one another or independently: education, homeownership (as a measure of wealth), income and occupation.

Examining census data with each of these measures offers a rough sense of the size of the black middle class. The 2000 U.S. Census reported that 16 percent of blacks (25 and older) have a bachelor's degree or higher. Forty-six percent live in an owner-occupied housing unit. The black median household income (in 1999 dollars) was $29,423, and 25 percent of the black employed are in management, professional and related occupations. For comparison purposes, 24 percent of the U.S. population (25 and older) as a whole have a bachelor's degree or higher. Sixty-six percent live in an owner-occupied housing unit. The median household income (in 1999 dollars) was $41,994, and 34 percent were in management, professional and related occupations.

Researchers widely agree that middle-class blacks have not been insulated from historical and persistent marginalization, discrimination and racism. Consequently, the black middle-class experience differs from that of the white middle class. Middle-class blacks live in less socioeconomically attractive neighborhoods and in close proximity to the black poor. Substantial wealth disparities relative to whites leave middle-class blacks with fewer assets to bequeath to the next generation. The extended family structure of middle-class blacks, which emphasizes a moral obligation and social responsibility to invest assets in their extended family and the larger black community, prevents assets accumulation for middle-class blacks. . . .

Recent Shifts in the Composition of the Black Middle Class

The composition of the black middle class is shifting. In 2000, 11 percent of black middle-class households with the householder in the 25- through 54-year-old range were SALAs, up

Black Singles Are Purchasing More Homes

In 2003, unmarried women were nearly twice as likely to buy homes as unmarried men. . . .

From 1997 to 2002, conventional mortgage loans to black women increased by 114 percent in metro Atlanta, a draw for middle-class blacks from across the nation. That growth greatly outpaced mortgage loans to white men and white women, which increased in the region by 35 percent and 26 percent, respectively. Mortgage growth in the region was highest among single black men, but they bought fewer homes than single black women.

Janet Frankston,
"Single Black Women Are Purchasing More Homes,"
San Diego Union-Tribune, July 11, 2004.

from 5 percent in 1980; the same pattern is apparent among younger households (25–44). This study clearly detects the presence of a Love Jones Cohort. Given the assumption that the Love Jones Cohort is a phenomenon of younger house-holders, we graph these changes in household percentages by middle-class status for households with householders ages 25 to 44. . . . In 2000, single and living alone householders made up 14 percent of middle-class black households. This means SALAs more than doubled their share of the black middle class, from 6 percent in 1980. Meanwhile, married-couple households with children are decreasing their share and for-merly married are retaining their share. Among households with householders ages 25–44, the proportion of middle-class households that were married-couple living without children remained virtually unchanged from 1980 to 2000. . . .

Married-couple households with children comprise the largest segment of the black middle class although they have been steadily declining since 1980. In 2000, the Love Jones Cohort, slightly edging out the formerly married households, made up the second largest segment of the black middle class. . . . SALA was the fastest growing black middle-class household with householders in the 25- through 44-year-old range between 1980 and 2000. If present trends persist, SALA is on track to become the household type accounting for the largest segment of the black middle class. . . .

Who Qualifies as Middle Class?

SALA households made continual strides from 1980 to 2000 in increasing their relative odds of acquiring middle-class status. In 2000, we find that married-couple households without children have greater odds of being middle class than married-couple households with children. We also find that single households with an adult and children have much lesser odds of being in the middle class than married-couple households with children. This pattern is also true in 1990. . . .

In 2000, female SALA households are about half as likely to qualify as black middle class as are married-couple households with a child; the difference between the odds ratios for these two households is statistically significant. In 2000, single female households living with an adult have slightly lower odds of being in the black middle class than married-couple households with a child. In 2000, male SALA households and those single households living with an adult have much lower odds of being middle class when compared with married-couple households living with a child. The formerly married female householders and those male householders have much lower odds of being middle class compared to married-couple households living with a child. A clear disparity exists between female SALA and those formerly married householders in relation to them being middle class when married-couple households living with a child are the referent group. This disparity is not evident among these same male householders. Regardless of whether a single householder with children is man or woman, this household type still reports the lowest odds of being middle class when compared with married-couple households living with a child. This model does suggest, however, that women living alone or with an adult (but not those formerly married) have greater odds than their male counterparts of acquiring middle-class status. . . .

In 2000, married-couple households without a child have greater odds of being in the black middle class than married-couple households with a child. . . . Out of all households, married-couple households without children consistently have the greatest odds of being middle class.

The Love Jones Cohort Feeds Black Middle-Class Growth

The Love Jones Cohort indeed exists. SALAs, one of the defining components of the Love Jones Cohort, are increasing their share of black households, and they are increasing their share of black middle-class households. Furthermore, the proportion of all black households that are SALA *and* middle class holds steady as the cohort ages, indicating this is not a short-lived phenomenon among younger individuals. Although SALAs still represent a relatively small percentage of the black middle class overall, among those ages 25–34 in 2000, SALAs account for roughly a quarter of black middle-class households.

In answer to the specific research questions, the data suggest that the black middle class continues to grow when examining black households with householders in the 25- to 54- and 25- to 44-year-old ranges, and that the Love Jones Cohort could be the leading cause of this growth. This study confirms that in 2000 nearly one in six black middle-class households with householders ages 25–44 was a SALA household, and close to one in four black middle-class households with a householder ages 25–34 were SALAs. A possible implication is that SALAs are on a trajectory to becoming the most prominent household within the black middle class if not the entire black community. Although this is a bold claim, these findings support this notion. Social scientists can no longer afford to overlook this group.

Our analysis positively illustrates that the Love Jones Cohort has maintained its household status of SALA and its socioeconomic status of black middle class for the past 20 years. Married-couple households have decreased their share of the black middle class during this same period. Thus the Love Jones Cohort is not only becoming the newest face of the black middle class, it may possibly become the most pronounced household type for this class group.

"An alarming number of today's black middle-class parents are themselves at high risk of falling down the economic ladder and bringing their children along with them."

Blacks Are at Risk of Falling Out of the Middle Class

Maya Payne Smart

Writer Maya Payne Smart focuses much of her research and work on business, lifestyle trends, and education. Economic adversity, she finds, hits the African American community harder than other groups. In the viewpoint that follows, she examines why the black middle class is vulnerable and why one generation's gains can be so quickly lost when the country's financial picture turns stormy. In her view, the black middle class does not possess the same educational or economic opportunities as its white counterpart, leaving it fragile in hard times. She insists that African Americans have to work for policy changes, create ladders to aid lower class blacks, and subscribe to new values if blacks are to continue their upward climb in American society.

Maya Payne Smart, "Life and Times of the Middle Class," *Black MBA Magazine*, vol. 11, Fall 2008, pp. 28–34. Reproduced by permission.

As you read, consider the following questions:

1. According to Smart, how many cents per dollar of white income do black middle-class workers possess?

2. In Karim Hutson's opinion—as quoted in Smart's viewpoint—what extra social responsibilities do educated, professional blacks have?

3. According to a Pew survey cited in Smart's viewpoint, what percentage of African Americans believe that blacks still have enough in common to be considered a race?

For many black families, remaining in the middle class is like walking a tightrope. The satisfaction they feel upon ascending to this height is tempered by the recognition of how far—and how fast—they can fall. They struggle to maintain their footing as economic woes and persistent racial inequality compete to knock them off-balance. Downward mobility for many is just a job loss or medical emergency away.

Black Children Are Slipping Out of the Middle Class

Research conducted by Julia Isaacs, the child and family policy fellow at the Brookings Institution, revealed that the children of black middle-income families are exceptionally vulnerable to falling into lower-income brackets. Comparing the incomes earned by parents in 1968 with those of their children 30 years later, she found that just 17 percent of black children born to parents earning between $49,000 and $65,000 in 2006 moved upward to higher earning levels, compared to more than a third of white children. Worse still, nearly half of black children of solidly middle-income parents fell to the bottom-income quintile, compared to the 16 percent of white children who hit rock bottom.

"Many middle-income black parents have seen their children's incomes fall below their own, and disturbingly high numbers of black children have fallen from the middle to the bottom of the income distribution," Isaacs reports. "Economic success in the parental generation—at least as measured by family income—does not appear to protect black children from future economic adversity the same way it protects white children."

This downward mobility amid the backdrop of tremendous civil rights gains is disturbing enough, but the black middle class's tenuous position has gotten even shakier given the current housing crisis and conservative policy environment. An alarming number of today's black middle-class parents are themselves at high risk of falling down the economic ladder and bringing their children along with them.

The Dangers That Beset the Black Middle Class

The middle-income designation obscures a broad array of financial, social, political, and even cultural factors that make black middle-class status peculiarly fragile. In fact, many middle-income blacks lack the degrees, occupational status and other attributes that many think of as middle class.

Black families are concentrated in the lower-income levels within the middle class, and even at equal income levels they tend to lag far behind whites in educational attainment and wealth accumulation—two factors that bolster one's ability to navigate tough economic times like these. Members of the black middle class have just 15 cents of wealth for every dollar their white counterparts possess and most of their wealth is held in their home or car equity.

Middle-class blacks are more likely to live in close proximity to high school dropouts and the unemployed than comparable whites. College-educated blacks frequently contend with worse schools and greater levels of crime, drug abuse, and urban decay in their neighborhoods. A disproportionate number of middle-income blacks work in blue-collar professions, which have been hit heavily in the current economic slump.

Recent research from the Institute on Assets and Social Policy at Brandeis University and Demos, a New York-based public policy research firm, found that only a quarter of black middle-class families have the assets, education and income after expenses and health insurance that is needed to maintain their middle-class status. One in three is at high risk of falling out of the class. Roughly 95 percent of black families don't have the net assets to cover their essential living expenses for three months if their income were interrupted, compared with 78 percent among the middle class as a whole. Just 2 percent could manage for nine months, compared with the already low national average of 13 percent. A full 68 percent of black middle-class households have no net financial assets at all.

Taken together, these factors describe a black middle class that is hanging on by the barest of threads. And it's not only this population that is hurt when households lose their economic footing—their families, neighborhoods and local economies feel the strain, too.

Funding Social Consciousness

In many cases, black professionals who have positioned themselves well in terms of education and earning power carry the additional weight of being a financial resource for less privileged members of their extended family.

Karim Hutson, the managing member of Genesis Companies, a New York-based real estate development and construction firm, says that he and his other black Harvard Business School graduates feel a responsibility to give back to their families, churches and communities. Having often grown up in economically adverse situations, they utilize their professional success to give back financially and through community service.

"As a young professional, I sit on four boards," Hutson says. "It is incredibly important to me that in all my professional and personal endeavors, I remain conscious of where I came from and help contribute positively to the community in every possible capacity."

Strengthening the economic standing of African Americans also would bolster the competitiveness of the cities where they reside. A study released by the Chicago Urban League posited that the city's economic advancement is intimately tied to that of its 1.1 million black residents. The report stated that greater economic inclusion would bolster per capita and household income, educational achievement, property values, tax receipts from tourism, and workforce productivity for the city at large.

"The city could expect to enjoy significant gains in GDP [gross domestic product] if the nearly $4 billion in revenues produced annually by African American–owned firms were to double or even triple," the report states. "Benefits such as these could be combined with traditional social services to reverse decades of slippage in African American economic vitality."

The Need for Policy Commitments

Policy efforts from boosting homeownership and savings rates to expanding educational access sound good, but new economic realities pose significant challenges. Predatory lending is systematically stripping tens of thousands of black households of home equity, their primary source of wealth. And lenders are running scared as fallout from the subprime mortgage debacle continues to ripple through the economy, making it even harder for families to buy regardless of creditworthiness. In the meantime, the cost of a college education is skyrocketing at three to four times the rate of inflation.

Roderick Harrison, a consultant with the Joint Center for Political and Economic Studies and an associate professor at

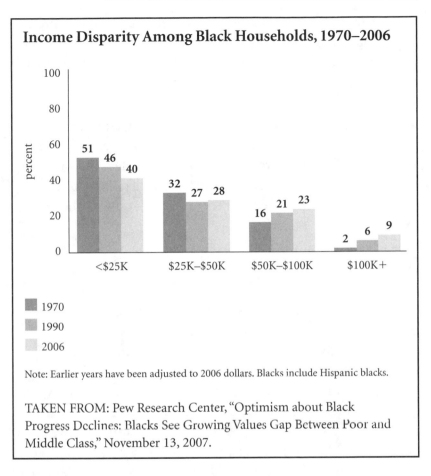

Income Disparity Among Black Households, 1970–2006

Note: Earlier years have been adjusted to 2006 dollars. Blacks include Hispanic blacks.

TAKEN FROM: Pew Research Center, "Optimism about Black Progress Declines: Blacks See Growing Values Gap Between Poor and Middle Class," November 13, 2007.

Howard University, says the black middle-income population's disproportionate number of blue-collar workers could prove devastating in this economy. "We could be facing a period where there could be serious losses of middle-class status and reversing the trend over the last four decades for the growth of the middle class," he says. "Even during the 1980s when growth was slow and incremental, we never had a drop in the percentage of blacks in the middle-income brackets."

He believes that policies must focus on both ends of the spectrum. Programs must be developed to provide the financial and academic support needed to increase the percentage of blacks who earn bachelor's degrees and to provide jobs for low-skilled, low-educated workers. "It was actually the so-called lousy jobs that had the greatest effect in reducing black poverty during the '90s," he says of the [Bill] Clinton-era job creation.

"We need to realize that not everybody will be able to get into telecommunications or high tech or whatever the latest fad is. There are people who need the restaurant job and for whom particularly we raise the minimum wage," he says. "For a lot of people, an eight-, nine- or ten-dollar job or two in a married couple means that they are not going to be raising their children in poverty."

Invest in Education

Mary Pattillo, a professor of sociology and African American studies at Northwestern University, says public policy fueled the expansion of the black middle class in the latter half of the 20th century. "After the major policy intervention of the 1950s to 1970s—school desegregation, the Civil Rights Act, the Fair Housing Act, affirmative action—any subsequent growth in the black middle class has been the result of overall economic growth as was seen in the 1990s under Clinton and before 9/11 [2001 terrorist attacks]," she explains.

Pattillo, the author of *Black on the Block: The Politics of Race and Class in the City* and *Black Picket Fences: Privilege and Peril Among the Black Middle Class*, advocates policy intervention to turn the tide. "In order to spur upward mobility among blacks, which still trails far behind whites, there needs to be investment in public education through college, as well as a commitment to affirmative action," she says. "The returns to a college education have grown tremendously since the 1970s and much of the income gap can be attributed to differences in educational attainment."

Indeed, history has shown that policy efforts that don't address discrimination along with opportunity fall short. The post-World War II policies that strengthened the middle class as a whole by expanding college education and homeownership didn't allow African Americans to ride as high as whites on the wave of economic progress.

Rethinking Class Values

Beyond policy changes, many say there's a role for black professionals to play in securing the economic future of black middle-income families and bolstering the possibility of intergenerational wealth transfer. And values have as much to do with it as economics.

Geoff Ratliff, the finance and accounting director of Habitat for Humanity–Newark, believes that all black people have an obligation to advocate for educational and occupational opportunities for the least fortunate. He sees a growing number of black professionals who are so focused on the day-to-day grind of competing in the workplace and providing for their families that they've lost sight of their broader responsibilities to the race. "We need to make an effort to reach back and help each other," he says. "I don't think that's happening at the level that it should be."

The University of Virginia graduate who also holds an MBA from St. Louis University says today's young professionals haven't experienced the kind of overt racism and segregation that forged strong ties among black people in their parents' generation regardless of income, education or occupation. "We are the first adult generation of African Americans who have not had a defining purpose or struggle like the civil rights movement to unify our race," he says. "The identity factors aren't forced upon us; we have to make the effort to unify ourselves."

This may be a hard sell for the increasing number of African Americans who have a hard time seeing themselves as connected to blacks on the other side of the class divide. In recent years, African Americans have begun to perceive a chasm between middle-class and poor blacks that goes beyond financial considerations. The differences are so pronounced that nearly 40 percent of African Americans surveyed by the Pew Research Center last year [2007] said that blacks can no longer be thought of as a single race. Just 53 percent said blacks still have enough in common to be considered a race.

More than 60 percent of the surveyed blacks said the values of middle-class and poor blacks have diverged in the last decade. Nearly a third said the two groups share "little" or "almost no" values in common. "Values" were defined as "things that people view as important or their general way of thinking." But describing these values in detail often proves controversial.

Providing Role Models

Lawrence Otis Graham, author of *Our Kind of People: Inside America's Black Upper Class*, has caught considerable flack for his efforts to identify and document the credentials and customs of the African American elite. Unapologetically, he believes that work like his has the power to uplift all black people by giving them a worthy model of success to emulate. In fact, his next book, *The Our Kind of People 800 Register*, intends to list the wealthiest, best-educated, and most socially prominent black families and individuals in America.

"It is important to draw the distinctions because we are not a monolith and we need to give our children permission to say, 'I want to be a member of the best and brightest'—not so that they can look down on other people, but so that they can say, 'I want to set my goals as high as any high-achieving white person would say,'" he explains.

According to Graham, no discussion of class distinctions is complete without reference to values and lifestyle. He says the black middle class should be defined in part by its emphasis on grooming its children for academic and professional excellence. He defines the black upper class by its success in transferring intergenerational wealth and long-standing affiliations with certain schools and social organizations.

"We have so much to fight against when it comes to our image and the way that we are portrayed," Graham says of African Americans. "We've embraced the stereotype that being ambitious or wealthy is to no longer be authentically black," he says. "We've embraced it so closely that it's hard to let go of it. This is why young black children are accused of trying to be white when they use good diction."

Efforts to Shore Up the Middle Class

The road from tenuous middle-class status to the upper class Graham chronicles is long and rife with economic and social challenges for African Americans, but it's hard to challenge the wisdom of pursuing higher education, wealth accumulation and cultural enrichment.

Several initiatives led by local and national organizations are under way to shore up the black middle class by providing financial education with an emphasis on debt reduction, household budgeting and long-term investment. Rising awareness of the precarious state of the black middle class, combined with education and effective government policy, will help. African Americans' history of resilience despite extreme economic disadvantage provides cause for optimism as well.

> *"Poor black parents rear their children very differently from the way middle-class parents do, and even by the time the kids are four years old, the results are extremely hard to change."*

Poor Parenting Is Keeping Many Black Children Out of the Middle Class

Kay S. Hymowitz

Kay S. Hymowitz recently authored the book Marriage and Caste in America: Separate and Unequal Families in a Post-Marital Age. *Several key ideas from the book are included in the following viewpoint, which examines the core differences in how middle-class and poor families raise their children. In Hymowitz's opinion, low-income black parents are generally less responsive to their children's needs and are less dogmatic about ensuring that their children strive for goals in education and in other aspects of their lives. She believes that emphasizing schoolwork and responsibilities to family and community can help poor black parents give more opportunities to their children so that the chil-*

Kay S. Hymowitz. "What's Holding Black Kids Back?" *City Journal*, vol. 15, Spring 2005, pp. 14–23. Copyright © 2005 The Manhattan Institute. Reproduced by permission.

dren might escape poverty in the future. Hymowitz is the William E. Simon Fellow at the Manhattan Institute, an independent research and educational public policy organization.

As you read, consider the following questions:

1. Why does Hymowitz contend that Head Start programs generally fail to improve the education of poor black children?

2. According to Hymowitz, in what ways—besides those directly related to poverty—do poor parents typically differ from middle-income parents in their methods of child rearing?

3. What is the "natural growth" parenting philosophy, as Hymowitz describes it?

In January, almost 2,000 people jammed the auditorium at Wayne County Community College in Detroit in order to hear [black comedian] Bill Cosby yell at them—there's really no other way to put it—for being bad parents. That was after a crowd had already filled a hall in Newark. And another in Springfield, Massachusetts. And another in Milwaukee. And yet another in Atlanta.

Had Cosby not gone into quarantine as the result of sexual-abuse charges that prosecutors say they are no longer pursuing, there's no question that thousands more poor black parents would have come to town-hall meetings, asking the comedian-activist to harangue them, too. They would have waited in line to hear Cosby say the same sort of thing he said in front of the NAACP [National Association for the Advancement of Colored People] on the 50th anniversary of the Supreme Court's *Brown* [desegregation] decision last May [2004] when he started his crusade: "The lower economic people are not holding up their end of the deal. These people are not parenting!" Or the litany he presented in a [November 2004] Paula Zahn interview: "You got to straighten up your house!

Straighten up your apartment! Straighten up your child!" Wearing a sweatshirt with the motto "Parent Power!" he doubtless would have blasted the "poverty pimps and victim pimps" who blame their children's plight on racial injustice. "Proper education has to begin at home. . . . We don't need another federal commission to study the problem. . . . What we need now is parents sitting down with children, overseeing homework, sending children off to school in the morning: well fed, rested, and ready to learn."

Passing the Correct Judgment

Now Bill Cosby is a big star and all, but at 67, he's not exactly [pop singer] Beyoncé. Why would people hang from the rafters in order to hear an aging sitcom dad accuse them of raising "knuckleheads"? The commentariat, black and white, sure didn't have an answer. "Billionaire Bashes Poor Blacks," the *New York Times* headlined columnist Barbara Ehrenreich's attack on Cosby's critique. *Newsweek* columnist Ellis Cose admitted that there was some truth to Cosby's charges, but objected, "The basic question is whether criticizing such behavior is enough to change it." Hip-hop entrepreneur Russell Simmons harrumphed an answer to Cose's question: "Judgment of the people in this situation is not helpful." In his Paula Zahn interview, Cosby told how ex-poet laureate Maya Angelou had chided him in similar terms: "You know, Bill, you're a very nice man, but you have a big mouth."

Well, that's the point, isn't it? Cosby was filling auditoriums precisely because he *has* a big mouth, because he *was* being judgmental. His blunt talk seemed a refreshing tonic to the sense that the standard bromides about the inner city's troubles weren't getting blacks very far. Forty years after the war on poverty began, about 30 percent of black children are still living in poverty. Those children face an even chance of dropping out of high school and, according to economist Thomas Hertz, a 42 percent chance of staying in the lowest income decile—far greater than the 17 percent of whites born at the bottom who stay there. After endless attempts at school reform and a gazillion dollars' worth of what policy makers call "interventions," just about everyone realizes—without minimizing the awfulness of ghetto schools—that the problem begins at home and begins early. Yet the assumption among black leaders and poverty experts has long been that you can't expect uneducated, highly stressed parents, often themselves poorly reared, to do all that much about it. Cosby is saying that they can.

And about that, he is right.

Educational Benefits Showed Little Reward

Let's start with a difficult truth behind Cosby's rant: 40 years and trillions of government dollars have not given black and white children equal chances. Put aside the question of the public schools for now; the problem begins way before children first go through their shabby doors. Black kids enter school significantly below their white peers in everything from vocabulary to number awareness to self-control. According to a 1998 National Center for Education Statistics survey of kindergarten teachers, black children are much less likely to show persistence in school tasks, to pay close attention in class, or to seem eager to learn new things than are their white counterparts; Hispanic children fall midway in between. As a 2002 book from the liberal Economic Policy Institute, *Inequality at the Starting Gate*, puts it, "[D]isadvantaged [disproportionately black] children start kindergarten with significantly lower cognitive skills than their more advantaged counterparts." Dismayingly, the sentence might have come straight from a government commission on poverty, circa 1964—before the war on poverty had spent a dime.

And what about Head Start, perhaps the best-known war on poverty campaign, which was supposed "to bring these kids to the starting line equal," as President [Lyndon B.]

Johnson put it at the time? Head Start rested on the reasonable assumption that crucial to fighting poverty was to compensate for what was—or, more to the point, was not—happening at home. If poor kids arrived at school less prepared than their more well-to-do counterparts, well, then, give them more of what those other kids were getting: more stories, building blocks, and puzzles, more talk, more edifying adult attention—as well as good nutrition and health care. Although in retrospect, the first Head Start program in the heady summer of 1965—designed to last all of eight weeks—was wildly unrealistic, the approach still made sense. Poor kids would get a concentrated injection of middle-class child rearing in preschool, and they would start school ready to learn, to achieve at the same rate as their better-off peers, and eventually to live as well as they did.

Except it didn't work out that way. As a lingering reminder of the hopes and idealism that surrounded the war on poverty, Head Start, with its annual budget of $6.8 billion, remains a sentimental favorite of the public and of Congress. But the truth is, from the first time they parsed the data, Head Start researchers found that while children sometimes enjoyed immediate gains in IQ and social competence, these improvements tended to fade by the time kids hit third grade. . . .

Poor Parenting Is Depriving Black Children

So why have we been able to make so little headway in improving the life chances of poor black children? One reason towers over all others, and it's the one Cosby was alluding to, however crudely, in his town-hall meetings: Poor black parents rear their children very differently from the way middle-class parents do, and even by the time the kids are four years old, the results are extremely hard to change. Academics and poverty mavens know this to be the case, though they try to soften the harshness of its implications. They point out—correctly—that poor parents say they want the same things for their kids that everyone does: a good job, a nice home, and a satisfying family life. They observe that poor parents don't have the money or the time or the psychological well-being to do a lot of the quasi-educational things that middle-class parents do with their young children, such as going to the circus or buying Legos. They argue that educational deprivation means that the poor don't know the best child-rearing methods; they have never taken Psych 101, nor have their friends presented them with copies of *What to Expect: The Toddler Years* at their baby showers.

But these explanations shy away from the one reason that renders others moot: Poor parents raise their kids differently, because they see being parents differently. They are not simply middle-class parents *manqué* [fallen short]; they have their own culture of child rearing, and—not to mince words—that culture is a recipe for more poverty. Without addressing that fact head-on, not much will ever chance.

Social scientists have long been aware of an immense gap in the way poor parents and middle-class parents, whatever their color, treat their children, including during the earliest years of life. On the most obvious level, middle-class parents read more to their kids, and they use a larger vocabulary, than poor parents do. They have more books and educational materials in the house; according to *Inequality at the Starting Gate*, the average white child entering kindergarten in 1998 had 93 books, while the average black child had fewer than half that number. All of that seems like what you would expect given that the poor have less money and lower levels of education.

But poor parents differ in ways that are less predictably the consequences of poverty or the lack of high school diplomas. Researchers find that low-income parents are more likely to spank or hit their children. They talk less to their kids and are more likely to give commands or prohibitions when they do talk: "Put that fork down!" rather than the more soccer-

Disrespecting Education in the Black Community

A lot of black youth now are anti-education and anti-intellectualism, who feel that getting an education is being white, is acting white. We never had that in previous generations, this is something new. I think this is very, very disconcerting that black youth are culturally adapting such postures when the high school dropout rate is so high, when they're going to jail at increasing rates, it's in fact really very high, and in jail about 70 percent of inmates have not graduated from high school. So [Bill] Cosby's plea around educating, parents really tending to their children, reading to them, teaching them how to speak standard English is well taken and very important.

Alvin Poussaint, as told to Ray Suarez and Ta-Nehisi Coates,
"Tough Talk," NewsHour with Jim Lehrer (transcript),
July 15, 2004. www.pbs.org/newshour.

mommish, "Why don't you give me that fork so that you don't get hurt?" In general, middle-class parents speak in ways designed to elicit responses from their children, pointing out objects they should notice and asking lots of questions: "That's a horse. What does a horsie say?" (or that middle-class mantra, "What's the magic word?"). Middle-class mothers also give more positive feedback: "That's right! Neigh! What a smart girl!" Poor parents do little of this. . . .

Middle-Class Families Have a Mission

In middle-class families, the child's development—emotional, social, and (these days, above all) cognitive—takes center stage. It is the family's raison d'être [reason for being], its state religion. It's the reason for that Mozart or Rafi tape in the morning and that bedtime story at night, for finding out all you can about a teacher in the fall and for Little League in the spring, for all the books, crib mobiles, trips to the museum, and limits on TV. It's the reason, even, for careful family planning; fewer children, properly spaced, allow parents to focus ample attention on each one. Just about everything that defines middle-class parenting—talking to a child, asking questions, reasoning rather than spanking—consciously aims at education or child development. In *The Family in the Modern Age*, sociologist Brigitte Berger traces how the nuclear family arose in large measure to provide the environment for the "family's great educational mission."

The Mission, as we'll call it, was not a plot against women. It was the answer to a problem newly introduced by modern life: How do you shape children into citizens in a democratic polity and self-disciplined, self-reliant, skilled workers in a complex economy? It didn't take all that much solicitude to prepare kids to survive in traditional, agricultural societies. That's not the case when it comes to training them to prosper in an individualistic, commercial, self-governing republic. "[I]n no other family system, do children play a more central role than in that of the conventional nuclear family," Berger writes. . . .

The Mission aims to pass on to the next generation the rich vision of human possibility inherent in the American project, and to enlist them into passing down that vision to yet another generation, in what sociologists used to call "the reproduction of society." What goes around, comes around.

The "Natural Growth" Attitude

You don't have to have a PhD to know that many poor parents have not signed up for the Mission, but some academics have added to our understanding of this fact. Annette Lareau, author of *Unequal Childhoods*—perhaps the most extensive comparative ethnography of poor and middle-class parents of school-age children—describes the child-rearing philosophy among the poor and much of the working class as "natural growth." Natural-growth believers are fatalists; they do not see their role as shaping the environment so that Little Princes or Princesses will develop their minds and talents, because they assume that these will unfold as they will. As long as a parent provides love, food, and safety, she is doing her job.

Inner-city parents are often intensely critical of their neighbors who "do nothin' for their kids," as one of Lareau's subjects puts it, but that criticism is pretty much limited to those who don't provide clean clothes or a regular dinner or who let their kids hang out too late at night. Talking or reading to a young child or taking him to the zoo are simply not cultural requirements. Christina Wray, a Michigan nurse working with the Nurse-Family Partnership (NFP), one of the most successful programs for poor, young first-time mothers, says that when she encourages these mothers to talk to their babies, they often reply, "Why would I talk to him? He can't answer me." Mothers describe playing with or cuddling a baby or toddler, obligatory in suburban homes, as "spoiling."

Natural-growth theory also helps explain why inner-city parents don't monitor their teenagers as closely as middle-class parents do. For middle-class Missionaries, the teenager is still developing his brain and talents; if anything, his parents' obligations intensify to incorporate 6 A.M. swim practices and late-evening play rehearsals. But according to natural-growth theory, a teenager is fully grown. Dawn Purdom, one of Christina Wray's colleagues in Michigan, says that the mothers of teenage daughters she sees are more likely to look like their high school friends than their parents. "They watch TV programs together, they listen to the same music, they talk about their sexual relationships. . . . It's not like one is a leader or a role model and the other is a follower. There are no boundaries like that."

The Need for Involved Parents

Obviously, race has nothing to do with whether people become natural-growth-theory parents or Missionaries. In *Unequal Childhoods*, Lareau describes the daily ministrations of a black couple, a lawyer and a corporate manager, to their only child, Alexander, that would make [*New York Times* domestic life columnist] Judith Warner blanch. The boy takes piano and guitar lessons, plays basketball and baseball, is in the school play and the church choir. "Daily life in the Williams house owes much of its pace and rhythm to Alexander's schedule," Lareau writes. The whole household is geared toward "developing Alexander." The first words out of both parents' mouths at the end of every day, no matter how long and stressful, are: "Have you started your homework?" or "What do you have to finish for tomorrow?" The fact that he has two married parents is an immense advantage for Alexander: Together, mother and father form a kind of conspiracy to develop him, a labor-intensive and emotionally demanding project difficult enough for two parents. Lareau's sample is extremely small, but surely it is no statistical accident that all of her middle-class children are growing up with their own two parents, while her poor children are growing up in homes without their fathers.

You could argue, of course, that the Mission simply costs too much for poor parents to enlist; Little League uniforms and piano lessons cost money, after all. But observers of the inner city have found numerous poor parents who seek out—and find—ways to do a lot of what middle-class parents do. They locate community centers or church groups with after-school activities. More important, they organize the household around school activities and homework. Unlike one of Lareau's poor subjects, who hardly responds when she hears that her son is not doing his homework—because "in her view it is up to the teachers to manage her son's education. That is their job, not hers"—plenty of poor parents not only say that education is important but actively "manage" their children's educations. DePaul University professor William A. Sampson sent trained observers into the homes of a number of poor black families in Evanston, Illinois—some with high-achieving children, some with low-achieving. Though the field workers didn't go in knowing which children were which, they quickly found that the high achievers had parents who intuitively understood the Mission.

These parents, usually married couples, imposed routines that reinforced the message that school came first, before distractions like television, friends, or video games. In the homes of low achievers, mothers came home from work and either didn't mention homework or quickly became distracted from the subject. Sampson's book only describes school-age children, so we don't know how these families differed when their children were infants or toddlers, but it's a good bet that the parents of high achievers did not start showing an interest in learning only the day their kids started kindergarten. In the ways that matter for children, these are "middle-class, lower-class families," Sampson explains in *Black Student Achievement*. "The neighborhood is not responsible for the difference. Neither is race. Neither is income." No, only the parents.

Designing Programs to Help Poor Parents

Knowing that middle-class parents better prepare kids for school, social scientists have designed an array of programs to encourage poor mothers to act more like middle-class mothers. And sometimes the programs have some modest impact. In a recent survey of the literature, Jeanne Brooks-Gunn enumerates studies showing various programs that have increased maternal sensitivity, reduced spanking, "improv[ed] parents' ability to assist in problem-solving activities," and taught mothers to ask questions and to initiate conversations about the books they read to their children.

Trouble is, such programs treat the parent not as a human being with a mind, a worldview, and values, but as a subject who performs a set of behaviors. They teach procedural parenting. David Burkam, a co-author of *Inequality at the Starting Gate*, explains, "The way that we [social scientists] try to make sense of the world is to break the world into small little bits and pieces and try to say which little piece is important." So they come up with a little piece that seems important, and that, not coincidentally, is directly observable and measurable—like, say, discipline—and they try to find a way to teach a poor mother to reason or give a time-out, rather than spank her child. They design an intervention, and they do the research to see if they have changed a mother's behavior and improved the child's situation. If the answer is yes, if there are "positive effects," the intervention is deemed a success and becomes part of the catalog of programs for improving children's chances.

Inspiring Better Parenting

But it should be clear by now that being a middle-class—or an upwardly mobile immigrant—mother or father does not mean simply performing a checklist of proper behaviors. It does not mean merely following procedures. It means believing on some intuitive level in the Mission and its larger framework of personal growth and fulfillment. In the case of poor parents, that means having an imagination of a better life, if not for you, then for your kids. That's what makes the difference.

It is this inner parent, the human being endowed with aspiration, capable of self-betterment and of reaching toward a better future, that Bill Cosby was trying to awaken in his notorious town-hall meetings. Cosby struck many as insufficiently sensitive to the challenges that the inner-city poor face. Perhaps. But the people pouring into his lectures were not looking for sympathy. They were looking for inspiration, a vision of a better self implicit in Cosby's chastisements. This is a self that procedural parenting ignores.

No one could reasonably expect Cosby's crusade to change much on its own. But as part of a broader cultural argument from the bully pulpits of government, churches, foundations, and academia, it is essential. It is at that point that interventions—and schooling—can have "positive effects" worth crowing about.

Periodical Bibliography

The following articles have been selected to supplement the diverse views presented in this chapter.

Elizabeth Aranda   "Struggles of Incorporation Among the Puerto Rican Middle Class," *Sociological Quarterly*, May 2007.

Vince Beiser   "Wild at Heart," *Sierra*, September/October 2007.

Ginia Bellafante   "On BET, Lifestyles of the Rich and Real," *New York Times*, March 23, 2009.

Albert S. Broussard   "Living Beyond the Dream: 40 Years After Dr. King," *Black Collegian*, January 2009.

José A. Cobas and Joe R. Feagin   "Language Oppression and Resistance: The Case of Middle Class Latinos in the United States," *Ethnic & Racial Studies*, February 2008.

Margaret Sauceda Curwen   "Visiting Room 501," *Phi Delta Kappan*, June 2009.

Michael Fletcher and Cynthia Gordy   "The Class War in Black America," *Essence*, May 2007.

Malik Miah   "Race and Class: Downturn Undermines Black 'Middle Class,'" *Against the Current*, March/April 2009.

New York Times Magazine   "G.M., Detroit and the Fall of the Black Middle Class," July 12, 2009.

Melvin L. Oliver and Thomas M. Shapiro   "Sub-prime as a Black Catastrophe," *American Prospect*, September 22, 2008.

Jody Agius Vallejo and Jennifer Lee   "Brown Picket Fences: The Immigrant Narrative and 'Giving Back' Among the Mexican-Origin Middle Class," *Ethnicities*, March 2009.

Kai Wright   "The Assault on the Black Middle Class," *American Prospect*, August 4, 2009.

 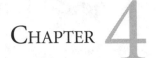

Is the American Middle Class in Decline?

Chapter Preface

In 1986, *Time* magazine reported on a phenomenon that had been troubling some U.S. economists, sociologists, and politicians since the early years of the decade: "The great American middle class, the provocateurs contend, is no longer so great. It is shrinking steadily, goes the theory, and shedding its members into the economic extremes of wealth and poverty." Stephen Koepp and his colleagues who wrote the *Time* piece said that those experts who warned that the country was dividing into haves and have-nots were mainly liberal and based their arguments on a collapsing industrial base. "Millions of citizens, they contend, have lost their middle-class jobs in aging industries like autos and steel and have plunged into the minimum-wage realm of floor mopping and hamburger flipping."

Since the 1980s, the worry over a shrinking middle class has grown. In 2009, the administration of President Barack Obama released its budget request to Congress, calling for a renewed commitment to strengthen the American economy. Obama's budget request warned that wealth was concentrated at the top tier of the class system and that "the opportunity for all Americans to get ahead, to enter the middle class, and to create a better life for their children [is] becom[ing] more and more elusive." The administration claimed that the failure of wages to keep pace with inflation and taxes has forced many Americans to sink into debt, trapping the middle class in a repayment cycle it cannot easily escape. "And some Americans have not been able to keep up, falling out of the middle class and into poverty," the administration lamented.

Not all experts, however, agree with the administration's predictions or the more widespread belief that the middle class is shrinking. Writing in *Forbes* in June 2009, Thomas F. Cooley, an economist and a dean of the New York University

School of Business, took issue with the claim that workers are not receiving the share of the economic pie that they deserve, while CEOs are getting fat off profits. "This is simply not true," Cooley retorts. Citing research done by economists Emmanuel Saez and Thomas Piketty, Cooley states that the share of the gross wealth of the nation has not changed much over the past sixty years for people earning between $104,000 and $383,000 (that is, the middle class and most business executives). What has changed is that incomes for the top 1 percent of earners has risen remarkably, indicating that a very few are making more money—because, in Saez and Piketty's view, they have the human capital to take advantage of improved technologies that bring greater wealth. Cooley adds that, of course, the wealth of the nation also expands, meaning that even if the percentage of wealth accumulated doesn't radically change, the dollar amount of that wealth does change. Or as Cooley writes, "The middle feels as if it has lost ground because of the extraordinary wealth accumulated by the very, very few. But that suggests that the pie is a fixed size, and that is clearly not the case."

In the following chapter, syndicated columnist Steve Chapman follows up Cooley's assessment by pointing out that the middle class in America has excess buying power, allowing it to acquire more luxuries than it has in the past. In Chapman's view, the middle class of today is better off than it has been in decades. Other commentators in the chapter, however, use their own measurements to gauge the health and well-being of the middle class, drawing differing conclusions and revealing how controversial the issue remains.

> *"A majority middle-class America was a relatively brief condition that existed between the 1930s and about 1980."*

The Middle Class Is Worse Off than in Past Decades

Tom Eblen

The middle class of America, long thought to be the majority of all Americans, does not enjoy the same prosperity it did in previous decades, argues Tom Eblen in the following viewpoint. Eblen combines statistics and expert commentary to support his view that as the rich have gotten richer and the poor have gotten poorer, the American middle class has shrunk and continues to decrease in numbers. Eblen believes that eventually the middle class will cease to exist unless the American public and politicians recognize that cooperation between classes is key to a strong middle class and United States. Eblen is a columnist for the Lexington Herald-Leader *newspaper in Lexington, Kentucky. He was previously a reporter and editor for the* Atlanta Journal-Constitution *and the Associated Press.*

As you read, consider the following questions:

1. Eblen attributes America's achievement of the "highest overall standard of living in the planet's history" to what factors?

2. According to Eblen, during what decades were Americans mostly middle class?

3. What conditions does Eblen believe fostered the creation of a large middle class in America following World War II?

Well, the economists finally made it official this week [the first in December 2008]: We're in a recession. And, guess what? They said it began a year ago.

If you're like the three-fourths of Americans who consider themselves to be "middle class," this probably didn't come as a surprise. Many people feel as if they've been losing economic ground for years. That's because many of them have been.

Middle Class Has Been Shrinking for Nearly Four Decades

America has been a generally prosperous nation since World War II, achieving the highest overall standard of living in the planet's history. The reasons are many, including advances in technology and global economic trends that have made goods cheap and available. Americans have been innovative, entrepreneurial, and they have worked hard. At times, the nation has made significant public investments in physical infrastructure, such as highways, and social infrastructure, such as schools.

But the pain being felt in this recession has brought new attention to a trend economists have been watching for years: The rich really are getting richer, the poor really are getting poorer and the middle class has been shrinking steadily since the late 1970s.

It's a reality that government policy makers and business leaders must deal with as they try to pull us out of this mess. The issue could be especially important for Kentuckians, who lag behind their fellow Americans in just about every measure of economic well-being.

At the Kentucky Long-Term Policy Research Center's annual conference November 20 [2008] in Covington, there was an interesting panel discussion about the shrinking middle class and what it means for Kentucky. The news, as you might expect, wasn't good.

"I see, basically, that middle class dissolving," said Ron Crouch, a sociologist who has headed the Kentucky State Data Center at the University of Louisville since 1988. "The issue is, it probably takes two incomes to make it in today's society."

Examining Americans' Incomes

Middle class is hard to define, but a basic measure is income. A year ago, a study by the nonpartisan Congressional Budget Office reported big disparities in the growth of after-tax household income between 1979 and 2005, as measured in 2005 dollars.

The study found that the poorest 20 percent of American households saw their annual income rise by an average of $900 over that quarter-century. The second-poorest 20 percent, by $4,800. The middle 20 percent, by $8,700.

Things were much different on the high end. The upper-middle 20 percent of households saw annual income increase by $16,000. And the richest fifth, by $76,500. Among the wealthiest 1 percent of households, average annual after-tax income rose by $745,100, from $326,400 to $1,071,500.

Panelist Terry Brooks, executive director of Kentucky Youth Advocates, said Kentucky ranks sixth-highest nationally in the disparity between its richest and poorest citizens and 13th in the disparity between middle- and upper-income people.

Most people define middle class more broadly than just income; it's more about a feeling of security, Brooks said. Do I feel secure in my job, my home, my health, my retirement and my assets' ability to weather a setback?

For example, if every member of a family doesn't have health insurance, "you're just one bad illness away from risk," Brooks said.

That could help explain why the Pew Research Center and the Gallup organization reported this year that 25 percent of Americans felt they hadn't moved forward economically in the past five years, and 31 percent felt they had fallen back. It was the worst result in a half-century of polling on that question. Attitudes are important, because confident consumers spend more, and consumer spending is two-thirds of all economic activity.

The Middle Class and America's Image

Being middle class is an idea Americans hold dear, which is why many people think of themselves as middle class when, in reality, they are either wealthy or poor. It's especially true for baby boomers, who grew up in the 1950s and 1960s, when most Americans really were middle class.

Paul Krugman, the *New York Times* columnist and Princeton University professor who recently won the Nobel Prize for economics, has written that, far from being the norm, a majority middle-class America was a relatively brief condition that existed between the 1930s and about 1980.

Over the next few months, we'll hear politicians and ideological warriors debate how to fix the economy and what role government should play in that. My guess is we'll hear less than in the recent past about making government smaller, privatizing Social Security and cutting taxes for the rich. After all, some of the pillars of capitalism are lining up for billions in taxpayer bailouts.

Middle-Class Families Finding Themselves Homeless

The district's mail came back unopened. That was the first sign.

When Karen Kunkel, homeless coordinator for Maryland's Charles County Public Schools, contacted the family that had lived in a large, suburban home, she heard a story that is becoming increasingly familiar.

"She started to cry," Kunkel says, recalling that first talk with the children's mother. "She said, 'We don't live there anymore.'" . . .

As the economy worsens and job losses mount, school officials are seeing more families like this, part of the changing face of homelessness. The "traditional" faces—chronically homeless single adults and families living well below the poverty line—are still there, to be sure, and their numbers are growing. But they are being joined by middle-class families that "never experienced homelessness, never expected to experience homelessness," says William Cohee, the Maryland Department of Education's homeless education coordinator.

Lawrence Hardy,
"The Changing Face of Homelessness,"
American School Board Journal, *June 2009.*

The huge post–World War II American middle class was created, in part, through public investment such as the GI Bill [for members of the U.S. armed forces], better public schools, affordable home mortgages, good highways, Social Security, and Medicare.

Growing the middle class and returning the economy to health again will require more public investment. And it will mean creating smart policies to address demographic trends such as an aging population and inequities among growing minority populations.

A strong middle class is central to America's self-image, but the way to keep it strong is hotly debated. Crouch breaks it down into two basic philosophies, which he describes as the John Wayne view and the *Little House on the Prairie* view. One symbolizes rugged individualism; the other, the idea of "take care of yourself, take care of your family, but also watch out for your neighbor."

"We've got to get off this idea that John Wayne is who we are in America," Crouch said. "Basically, we're a country which was built on people helping each other. This society cannot afford to have winners and losers. We've got to make everyone a winner."

> *"Thanks to American capitalism, ordinary workers and families are better off today than they were a decade or a generation ago."*

The Middle Class Is Better Off than in Past Decades

Steve Chapman

Steve Chapman, a conservative commentator who writes for the Chicago Tribune *with syndicated columns appearing in newspapers nationwide, argues in the following viewpoint that while the media and Democrats propagate the message that the middle class is in decline, the opposite is actually true. Instead of facing a decline in wages and lower standards of living, Chapman claims that working Americans and their families are actually earning higher wages than thirty years ago. In addition, he cites data showing that they are spending their money on more goods to improve their living conditions. Chapman acknowledges that some people have lost their jobs in the recent economic upheaval, but maintains a positive outlook on American capitalism's ability to foster growth and economic prosperity for U.S. citizens.*

Steve Chapman, "Obama's Economic Mythology: Is the Middle Class Really in Decline?" Reason.com, October 30, 2008. Copyright © 2008 by Reason Foundation, 3415 S. Sepulveda Blvd., Suite 400, Los Angeles, CA 90034, www.reason.com. Reproduced by permission.

As you read, consider the following questions:

1. According to Chapman's numbers, how many more Wal-Mart stores are open in America today compared with the number open in 1988?

2. What are some of the "fringe benefits" that Chapman claims traditional earnings figures omit?

3. Based on the study conducted by economist Terry Fitzgerald and cited by Chapman, after accounting for fringe benefits and changing American family size, by what percentage range have median wages increased from 1976 to 2006?

If you're at a Catholic shrine, it's a good idea to show respect for the Virgin Mary. In New York, a Yankees cap will make you look right at home. And among a Democratic crowd, you can never go wrong by lamenting the decline of the middle class and the stagnation of wages.

I don't have to tell Barack Obama. He makes a habit of claiming that "wages are shrinking," working families have lost ground, and the country desperately needs his "Rescue Plan for the Middle Class." His economic program rests on the unshakable conviction that everyone except the wealthy is doing worse and worse all the time. He will find sympathetic ears among Democrats in Congress, where never is heard an encouraging word.

Media Exaggerating Economic Decline

In the midst of alarming headlines, it's easy to persuade people that things are worse than they used to be. The only problem is that aside from the transitory effects of the current turmoil, they aren't.

Even on that front, things are better than advertised. For nearly a year, we've been told that the economy is on the verge, if not the thick, of a painful recession. But the traditional definition of a recession is two consecutive quarters of negative growth—and we have yet to endure even one such quarter. In the second quarter [2008], the economy grew at a brisk 33 percent rate, which is the opposite of what happens in a downturn.

Given all the fallout from the housing bust and the mortgage meltdown, things may look worse when the data emerge for the third quarter. But they won't change the actual long-run picture on how most people are faring in the modern economy—which is much better than we have been led to believe.

American Workers' Wages and Spending Are Increasing

That is not really surprising. Everywhere you look, you see Americans shopping and buying. Vast expanses of land that used to harbor corn or cattle now provide a home for shopping centers that go on forever. In 1988, Wal-Mart had 1,200 stores. Today, it has 3,800. Americans bought 24 percent more new cars and trucks in 2007 than in 1990.

All sorts of products that didn't exist a generation ago are now commonplace even in humble neighborhoods—personal computers, cell phones, high-definition TVs, Polartec jackets, digital cameras, Starbucks coffee, and more. If their incomes are steadily falling, how do Americans cart home so much stuff?

Terry Fitzgerald, a senior economist at the Federal Reserve Bank of Minneapolis, says the answer is simple. Far from declining, he writes, "the economic compensation for work for middle Americans has risen significantly over the past 30 years."

The mistake made by the School of Gloom is looking only at wages, narrowly defined. According to the Bureau of Labor Statistics, average hourly earnings of production and nonsupervisory workers, adjusted for inflation, fell by 4 percent be-

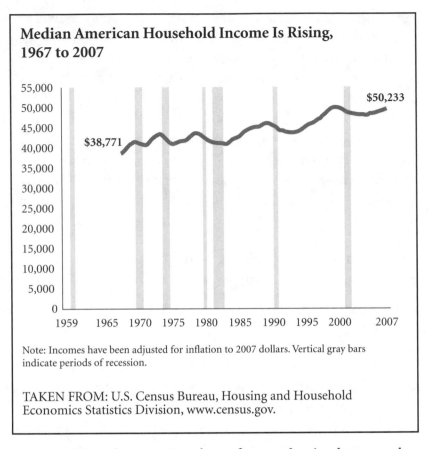

Median American Household Income Is Rising, 1967 to 2007

Note: Incomes have been adjusted for inflation to 2007 dollars. Vertical gray bars indicate periods of recession.

TAKEN FROM: U.S. Census Bureau, Housing and Household Economics Statistics Division, www.census.gov.

tween 1975 and 2005. But those figures deceive because they omit fringe benefits like health insurance, pensions, and paid leave, which make up a bigger share of total compensation than before. The numbers also rely on a mismeasure of inflation.

When those flaws are corrected, a very different trend leaps off the page. Median wages, says Fitzgerald, rose 28 percent between 1975 and 2005. Nor were the gains restricted to [Microsoft founder] Bill Gates and [fictional pop superstar] Hannah Montana: Significant gains occurred in the middle as well.

The same pattern holds for households. The figures that suggest families are struggling to stay even overlook some types of income, and they don't account for the fact that households have gotten smaller on average. After accounting for such things, Fitzgerald found that "inflation-adjusted median household income for most household types increased by roughly 44 percent to 62 percent from 1976 to 2006."

Capitalism Helps Americans Prosper

None of this alters the fact that some people have done worse. Domestic and global competition, which raise living standards, also spell trouble for many companies and workers. A 50-year-old who loses a $30-an-hour job on the Chevy assembly line may never find anything comparable. But the steady, broad rise in living standards makes it clear that—at least until recent months—our economy consistently spawns more good jobs than it destroys.

Thanks to American capitalism, ordinary workers and families are better off today than they were a decade or a generation ago. In the midst of scary economic times, that's a heartening fact to keep in mind. Even if certain Democrats would rather you didn't.

| "I believe our middle class has suffered in silence for far too long, and it simply cannot afford to suffer or be silent for much longer."

Big Business and Big Government Are Devastating the Middle Class

Lou Dobbs

In the viewpoint that follows, Lou Dobbs argues that big business and big government have together waged a war against the middle class, ignoring the rights of this group as well as the problems that these people are facing. Dobbs is unwavering in his critique of corporate influence over the government, and he contends that the politicians who are bending to the interests of corporations have become disinterested in their constituents' well-being, resulting in a dysfunctional government. Dobbs worries that if the American people do not take action soon, the middle class will remain subject to political power of big business and the indifference of the American government. Dobbs was the anchor and managing editor of Lou Dobbs Tonight, *a political,*

*economic, and social commentary program broadcast on CNN
until November 2009; he is also the author of numerous books
including* Independents Day: Awakening the American Spirit.

As you read, consider the following questions:

1. Dobbs believes that corporations in America exert their
   power over the American political parties using what
   means?

2. What are some of the issues and legislation that Dobbs
   charges corporate America with influencing and in some
   cases even writing?

3. According to Dobbs, why did he change the name of his
   program chronicling the problems of the middle class to
   "War on the Middle Class"?

George W. Bush claimed through two presidential campaigns that America has become the "ownership society."
I couldn't agree more. America has become a society owned
by corporations and a political system dominated by corporate and special interests, and directed by elites who are hos-
tile—or at best indifferent—to the interests of working men
and women of the middle class and their families.

Americans Are Ceding Control of the Government to Corporations

Corporate America holds dominion over the Republican and
Democratic parties through campaign contributions, armies
of lobbyists that have swamped Washington, and control of
political and economic think tanks and media. What was for
almost two hundred years a government of the people has become a government of corporations, and the consent of the
governed is now little more than a quaint rubric of our Dec-
laration of Independence, honored as a perfunctory exercise

in artifice, and practiced every two to four years in midterm and presidential elections in which only about half of our eligible voters go to the polls.

We stand on the brink of being judged by future historians as the generation that failed to heed Abraham Lincoln's call to assure that the "government of the people, by the people, for the people, shall not perish from the earth."

There is almost no countervailing influence in our society to mitigate, even at the margins, the awesome and all but total corporate ownership of our political system. Labor unions are nearing extinction, and those that survive are in the midst of internal leadership struggles to find relevance in our economy and our society. Most of our universities are rarely, if ever, bastions of independent thinking, social scholarship, and activism. Instead they are dependent and rely upon either the federal government or the favor of corporations and the wealthy for funding their very existences. Our churches are in decline and tend to expend their political energy on issues such as gay marriage and highly amorphous "family values" rather than on the relevant causes of our time, including the preservation of our traditional national values of independence, equality, personal freedom, the common good, and our national interest. Isn't preserving the American dream, and fighting back against those forces that would diminish or destroy it, a worthy cause for our traditional institutions and to all of us who care deeply about our great democracy and way of life?

No Longer a Government for the People

Most alarmingly, our federal government has become so dysfunctional that it no longer serves well the needs of the people, nor do our elected officials assert the common good against the power of money and capital.

No one believes more strongly than I do in our free enterprise democracy, or in the importance of capitalism as the driving force of our economy. At the same time, I also strongly reject unfettered capitalism, and those forces that now rampant corporatism has arrayed against our middle class and those who aspire to be part of it.

The title of this book reflects an evolution in my understanding of our failed public policies, business practices, and politics over the past five years, and of their disastrous impact on the single largest group or people in this country—our middle class. My understanding has, admittedly, evolved far too slowly, and occasionally only haltingly—especially when I consider that the result of those failed policies, practices, and politics are now so painfully obvious: Middle-class working men and women and their families have been devastated.

In this conflict, the middle class is not collateral damage. Working men and women are not innocent bystanders in a great national accident. Our political, business, and academic elites are waging an outright war on Americans, and I doubt the middle class can survive the continued assault by forces unleashed over the past five years if they go on unchecked.

Consequences of the Government-Corporate Partnership

Whether the issue is a total lack of border security, an illegal immigration crisis, taxation, education, or jobs, big business and big government are unchecked in their attacks on the common good. Most of our elected officials, whether Democrat or Republican, have been bought and paid for through campaign donations from corporate lobbyists and other special interest groups. We've reached a stage where lobbyists no longer merely influence legislation but write the actual language of what becomes law.

The Bankruptcy Abuse Prevention and Consumer Protection Act of 2005 is only one such example. Credit card, banking, and other financial institutions all but wrote this measure. As a law, it now means that many middle-class families cannot turn to the protection of bankruptcy—even though the leading cause of personal bankruptcy is the medical and health care costs incurred by catastrophic illness.

In conjunction with the Bush administration's unwavering commitment to faith-based economics and free trade at any cost, the effect of its failed public policies has been draconian. Our unrepresentative Congress has actually cheered on corporate America's business practices—practices that have destroyed millions of well-paying middle-class jobs, and continue to do so. We are witnessing something that would have been unimaginable a quarter century ago: the emergence of a House of Representatives and a Senate that ignore the will of the majority of Americans, the middle class. Politicians have become viciously and vacuously partisan, and contemptuous of their constituencies. These forces are committed to a world order that views national sovereignty and borders as inconvenient impediments to trade and commerce, and our citizens as nothing more than consumers or units of labor in a global marketplace. That ideology has damaged, perhaps irreversibly, our manufacturing base as a result of the corporate offshoring of production facilities and the outsourcing of jobs to overseas cheap labor markets.

Each night, as I conclude my nightly broadcast on CNN, I have the gut-sick feeling that we have chronicled another twenty-four hours in the decline of our great democratic republic and the bankrupting of our free enterprise economy. Almost every night it seems we report on the erosion of individual rights and individual liberty, on ever bolder attempts by political and business elites to define what America now means, and on actions of elected officials, corporate leaders, and special interests who seemingly are determined to deny millions of Americans the same economic and educational opportunities that previous generations enjoyed.

The War on the Middle Class

A few years ago, on *Lou Dobbs Tonight* [the author's show broadcast on CNN], we began reporting on the economic challenges facing most Americans in a series called "The Middle-Class Squeeze," which initially focused on health care, job losses in manufacturing, and the corporate outsourcing of jobs. In 2004, the [Senator John] Kerry [presidential] campaign even adopted "The Middle-Class Squeeze" as a designation for some of the senator's policy positions. By the end of that election year, we had escalated our coverage, and changed the title of the series to "Assault on the Middle Class." The economy had finally started creating jobs, but they were low-paying ones; middle-class jobs were still being shipped overseas. Those who lost their positions were finding new work, but slowly, and they were forced to accept 20 to 25 percent less in wages or salary. At the same time, public education, despite the No Child Left Behind Act [federal legislation enacted in 2002 with the goal of improving the education system in America by focusing on testing and accountability] (or perhaps because of it, as critics maintain), was failing millions of our students.

By now it had become evident to me that the problems beleaguering the middle class were about more than the erosion of jobs and pay, health care, and education. The issue was bigger than any of us could have imagined. When the realization that that was the case finally took hold last year, the title of our ongoing series was changed to "War on the Middle Class."

Make no mistake: This *is* an outright war. To call it anything less is a disservice to the truth and to the American people. The mass capitulation of most Americans to political correctness over the past two decades has frequently provoked me to forgo gentle and indirect language in favor of simpler and more direct statements of meaning. I'm biased in my preference for direct language, but I'm convinced there is no other way to address the most critical issues facing the country. . . .

Inequality in CEOs' and Middle-Class Workers' Pay

The American dream is one of upward mobility. We believe that if you work hard and play by the rules, you should be able to provide for your family and ensure that your children have greater opportunity than you were afforded. But today, the dream of true upward mobility has been limited to a select class of corporate executives while the dreams of middle-class families have been deferred. Corporate CEOs [chief executive officers] have enjoyed record levels of compensation and corporations have seen record profits, as more and more middle-class Americans are experiencing stagnant wages and vanishing benefits. This expanding inequality is not the American dream.

John Alexander Burton and Christian E. Weller,
"Supersize This: How CEO Pay Took Off
While America's Middle Class Struggled,"
Center for American Progress, May 2005.
www.americanprogress.org

Time to Defend the Middle Class

If ever there were a time for truth in America, it is now. For more than two hundred years, the American middle class has been the core of a work ethic, a tradition of values, and a belief that every citizen is an important part of a greater good. This heritage has made the United States a unique nation with shared goals and ideals. Our middle class is America's foundation, and it is in its hearts and minds that the ideal of America is held strongest and brightest.

But ours is becoming increasingly a divided society—a society of haves and have-nots, educated and uneducated, rich and poor. The rich have gotten richer while working people have gotten poorer. We must also recognize that our public education system is failing, that there are far fewer well-paying jobs for our workers, that the middle class is hardly represented in government, and that our community and national values are increasingly challenged by corporatism, consumerism, and ethnocentric multiculturalism.

Preserving the American Dream

At a time when our nation should be investing strongly in our middle class, dramatically improving poor schools, rebuilding our manufacturing base, and restoring and refurbishing our infrastructure throughout the country, we are allowing our biggest businesses to ignore their social responsibilities and our federal government to squander hundreds of billions of dollars and accumulate enormous debts—debts that will fall upon our children. While corporations are paying lower taxes than ever before, and tax breaks for the wealthy are expanded, the middle class is forced to shoulder ever more of the tax burden—even as American working men and women are working harder than ever simply to keep their jobs, and they are working longer hours at reduced pay with fewer benefits.

The people who built this country find themselves employed by companies that seem hell-bent on sending their jobs overseas to cut costs and payroll, and electing those representatives who ignore failing public schools and ever more expensive health care. They are, in short, becoming a class of people with uncertain job prospects, insecure financial futures, and the likelihood of a severely reduced standard of living. Making matters worse is the fact that, as a nation, we seem to be in the grip of a national ennui, a numb and passive acceptance of the status quo.

In my opinion we are on the verge of not only losing our government of the people, for the people, and by the people, but also standing idly by while the American dream becomes a national nightmare for all of us.

The Middle Class Must Reclaim Control of the Government

Our nation was built by working people who are at once the producers, the consumers, the taxpayers, and the electorate. They are individual contributors to our economy and have always cherished the principle that is the bedrock of democracy, the principle that every single vote counts. Individual rights and responsibilities are the core of America, both two hundred years ago when we were a country of only four million people and today, when we're three hundred million strong. But today we live in a postmodern society in which we've allowed interdependence to overpower individualism. The essential respect for the importance of the rights of the individual is eroding in America.

Americans are still the richest—in every sense of the word—people on Earth, with more guaranteed freedoms, more wealth, and more opportunity than anywhere else on the planet. Yet, in the past four decades, I think many of us have lost sight not only of who we are, but also of the powerful ideas that are the source of our traditions and our values. We have allowed the elites to subvert the principles of free markets and a democratic society, and to establish the lie that the unfettered growth of our economic system is far more important than the preservation of our political system.

I believe our middle class has suffered in silence for far too long, and it simply cannot afford to suffer or be silent for much longer. Hardworking Americans have not spoken out about their increasingly marginalized role in this society, and as a consequence they've all but lost their voice. Without that strong, clear, and vibrant voice, all the major decisions about America and our future will be made by the elites of government, big business, and special interests. Those elites treasure your silence, as it enables them to claim America's future for their own.

If we are to have the America you and I want, and the one we and our children deserve, we must resolutely face these challenges to our way of life. And we must do so now.

> "The United States has promoted the worldwide exchange of commodities like no other nation, and the result is that their local industry has begun to be eroded."

Globalization Is Devastating the Middle Class

Gabor Steingart

Globalization is a phenomenon whereby national societies and economies become ever more intertwined and interdependent through the open trade of goods and services, foreign investment, immigration, and technological advancement. While many have benefited from this exchange, in the viewpoint that follows, Gabor Steingart maintains that the United States economy has suffered from globalization. He contends that even as a handful of American citizens have profited greatly from partaking in expanded trade, the majority of Americans, specifically the middle class, have lost their jobs to outsourcing and the relocation of manufacturing plants. He predicts that as the country continues to import more products annually than it exports, the losses will increase and place additional burden on the middle class. Originally from Germany, Steingart is senior correspondent in Wash-

Gabor Steingart, "America's Middle Class Has Become Globalization's Loser," Spiegel Online, October 24, 2006. © Spiegel Online 2006. Reproduced by permission.

ington, D.C., for the German news magazine Der Spiegel, *and he is the author of numerous international best sellers including* The War for Wealth: The True Story of Globalization, or Why the Flat World Is Broken.

As you read, consider the following questions:

1. Why, according to Steingart, are the three characteristics that he identifies as America's greatest strengths also its greatest weaknesses?

2. How did the U.S. economy change at the end of the 1970s, according to the congressional report cited by Steingart?

3. How much was the U.S. trade deficit with China, Japan, and Europe in 2005, according to Steingart?

There are essentially three exclusive characteristics whose simultaneous development have served as the foundations of the United States' success up until now—and they only appear in this particular combination in America. They are not only the country's biggest strengths, but also its greatest weaknesses. It's worth scrutinizing them more closely.

Characteristics Unique to America

First, nowhere in the world can you find such a high concentration of optimism and daring. America is the country that strives hardest for what is new—not just since yesterday (like Eastern Europeans) and not just for the last three decades (like the Chinese); rather from the very instant settlers began arriving. Unabashed curiosity seems to be hardwired into the nation's genetic code.

The steady influx of the adventurous and hardworking—which helped increase the country's labor force by about 44 million people since 1980 alone and continues today—ensures a constant replenishment of daring. After all, it's not just the additional people that make the difference. The mere addition of 17 million people into Germany following reunification in 1990—newcomers more concerned with preserving their guaranteed rights than with making the extraordinary effort necessary for success—did nothing to foster the kind of daring you see in the United States. Indeed, the result was exactly the opposite, and it has been a painful lesson for Germany.

Second, the United States is radically global. Its very origins—in the rebellious citizens from every country in the world who assembled on the territory that is now the United States—mark its people as true children of the world. Former German Chancellor Helmut Schmidt calls the Founding Fathers of the United States a "vital elite," one that continues to pass down its genes to this very day. Their language is dominant, having marginalized Spanish and French during the second half of the past century. Their everyday culture—from the T-shirt and rock 'n' roll to e-mail—has peacefully colonized half the world. And from the very beginning, US corporations were eager to venture abroad in order to trade and set up production sites in other countries. Multinational corporations may not have been a US invention, but they became its specialty.

Third, the United States is the only nation on earth that can do business globally in its own currency. Indeed, the dollar has established itself as the world's currency. Whoever wants to own it has to purchase it in the United States. All important decisions about the quantity of cash that circulates or the setting of interest rates are made within the nation's borders, which guarantees a maximum degree of national independence. It's American blood that flows through the veins of the global economy. Almost half of all business deals are closed using dollars as the currency, and two-thirds of all currency reserves are held in dollars. Charles de Gaulle, who was president of France after World War II, admired this "exorbitant privilege" even then.

Self-Imposed Vulnerabilities

But there is a flip side to the coin. First, Americans are so optimistic that they often blur the line between optimism and naiveté. Public, private, and corporate debt far exceeds any previously known dimensions.

Forever piously trusting in a future rosier than the present, millions of households are borrowing so much money that they end up endangering the very future they're looking forward to. The lower and middle classes have practically given up on putting aside any savings. They're going into the 21st century like a poverty-stricken, third-world family, living from hand to mouth without any financial reserves whatsoever.

Second, globalization is striking back. The United States has promoted the worldwide exchange of commodities like no other nation, and the result is that their local industry has begun to be eroded. Some production sectors—such as the furniture industry, consumer electronics, many automobile part suppliers, and now computer manufacturers—have left the country for good. In the recent past, free trade has primarily benefited the very rival states that are now mounting an economic offensive on the United States—and which have cut off a large slice of America's global market share for themselves.

Third, the dollar doesn't just strengthen the United States; it also makes it vulnerable. The government has pumped its currency into the world economy so vigorously that the dollar can now be brought to the point of collapse by external forces—such as those in Beijing, for example. [Former] US president Bill Clinton spoke of a "strategic partnership." [Former] president George W. Bush would later speak of a "strategic rivalry." They meant the same thing. There's a form of dependence that obliges economic actors to cooperate in normal times. But when times change, there is the temptation to engage in a show of strength.

A Citizenry Detached from Its Country's Wealth

Make no mistake about it: At the start of the new century, the United States is still a superpower. But it is a superpower that faces tough competition from outside and difficulties within. The feedback effects involved in globalization are especially intense for the US economy—so much so that large parts of the US workforce are now standing with their backs against the wall.

The rise of Asia has only led to a relative decline of the US national economy. At least so far. But for many blue- and white-collar workers, this decline is already absolute because they have less of everything than they used to. They possess less money, they are shown less respect in society and their chances for climbing up the social ladder have deteriorated dramatically. They're the losers in the world war for wealth. But while that may be their fate, they cannot be faulted for it. And it's certainly not a private affair. Every nation has to face uncomfortable questions when an ever-larger part of its citizenry is delinked from the nation's overall wealth. This is all the more true of a society that has made the pursuit of happiness a fundamental right.

Globalization Leads to a Shift in Capital

On October 28, 1998, the US Congress established a commission that brought together highly respected experts to examine the effects of the country's trade deficit and the withering away of industrial labor. Donald Rumsfeld, [then] US defense secretary, then US Trade Representative Robert Zoellick, Anne Krueger, the number two at the International Monetary Fund (IMF) and Massachusetts Institute of Technology (MIT) professor Lester Thurow provided their assessment of the situation at the behest of the president.

Things were going swimmingly for the Americans until the end of the 1970s, the commission report concluded. Family incomes grew virtually at the same rate in all sections of the population during the first three decades after World War II, with those of the poor growing slightly faster. The lowest fifth of US society saw a 120 percent increase in incomes, the second fifth 101 percent, the third 107 percent, the fourth 114 percent and the fifth 94 percent. It was as if the American dream had manifested itself in statistics.

But then the trend reversed, and not just in the United States. Japan had awakened, and global trade had shifted directions. Capitalists left their home turf and went looking for suitable locations to invest in. Direct investment abroad—which had been more or less in harmony with exports until then—rose dramatically.

Until then, investment abroad had served mainly to boost the export of German, US, or French products. But then factories themselves began to be relocated, mainly to cut manufacturing costs. Production for the world market became increasingly global itself, which led to a redistribution of capital and labor. Global production increased by a solid 100 percent between 1985 and 1995. But direct investment abroad increased by 400 percent during the same time period. Capital's new mobility began to make the other factor of production, labor, restless, too.

The End of the US Economy's Golden Age

The new jobs were created elsewhere, which had to have an effect on family income in the United States. Within the next two decades, the income of the lowest fifth sank by 1.4 percent. The second fifth still managed to gain by 6.2 percent, the third by 11.1 percent and the fourth by 19 percent. At the tip of the pyramid—where the promoters and planners of globalization reside, and those who profit most from it—income gains climbed by 42 percent.

The US national economy clearly bears the signs of this break with its golden age, when the country produced pros-

The Global Middle Class Is Expanding

The [members of the] middle class get a lot of attention, particularly in developed economies. They are held up frequently as the engine of growth, the bastion of social values and the arbiter of elections. And in many countries, the commentary increasingly paints the picture of an embattled and shrinking middle class, fighting against a rising tide of inequality.

Within much of the developed world, parts of this picture are justified and the last decade has seen income disparities increase in a range of places. But *globally*, the opposite is true. In fact . . . , we are in the middle of an unprecedented explosion in what might be considered a 'world middle class', which we define as those with incomes between $6,000 and $30,000 in PPP terms [purchasing power parity, an economic theory that is useful when making comparisons between countries' economies because it minimizes the impact of currency exchange rates and fluctuations]. And global income distribution is getting narrower, not wider.

This story of what we call the 'Expanding Middle' is set to continue, if not accelerate, over the next two decades and is likely to be critical to how the world is changing.

Dominic Wilson and Raluca Dragusanu,
"The Expanding Middle: The Exploding
Middle Class and Falling Global Inequality,"
Goldman Sachs Global Economics Paper, no. 170,
July 7, 2008.

perity for almost everyone. Until the 1970s, the productive core of the country burned with such a fiery light that it illuminated the entire world. The United States provided dollars and products for everyone. The American empire's nuclear power helped in the reconstruction of war-torn Europe and Japan. The United States was the world's greatest net exporter and greatest creditor for four decades. Everything went just the way the economy textbooks said it should: The world's wealthiest nation pumped money and products into the poorer states. The United States used the energy from its own productive core to make other countries glow or at least glimmer. It was indisputably the world's center of power, a source of energy that radiated out in all directions.

US capital was at home everywhere in the world, even without military backing. Many experienced this state of affairs as a blessing, some as a curse. Either way, it was good business for the United States: At the peak of its economic power, the West's leading nation disposed of assets abroad whose net value amounted to 13 percent of its GNP [gross national product, which measures the total value of goods and services produced by the citizens of a country in both domestic and international locations]. To put it differently: The country's productive core had expanded so dramatically that it opened up branches and subsidiaries all over the world.

This United States Imports More than It Exports

This undoubtedly superior United States doesn't exist anymore. As a center of power, it is still more powerful than others, but for some years now that energy has been flowing in the opposite direction. Today, Asian, Latin American, and European nations are also playing a role in the United States' productive core. The world's greatest exporter became its greatest importer. The most important creditor became the most important debtor. Today, foreigners dispose of assets in the United States with a net value of $2.5 trillion, or 21 percent of gross domestic product. Nine percent of shares, 17 percent of corporate bonds and 24 percent of government bonds are held by foreigners.

Neither laziness nor the obvious American penchant for consumerism can be blamed for this changed reality in America. US industry—or at least what little is left of it—is responsible. In the span of only a few decades, US industry has shrunken to half what it once was. It makes up only 17 percent of the country's GDP [gross domestic product, which measures the total value of goods and services produced by the citizens of a country within that country], compared to 26 percent in Europe.

Every important national economy in the world now exports products to the United States without purchasing an equivalent amount of US goods in return. The US trade deficit with China was about $200 billion dollars in 2005; it was a solid $80 billion with Japan; and more than $120 billion with Europe. The United States can't even achieve a surplus in its trade with less developed national economies like those of Ukraine and Russia. Every day, container-laden ships arrive in the United States—and after they unload their wares at American ports, many return home empty.

Those looking for something good to say about the superpower won't find it in the trade balance. The growing imbalance can't be attributed to natural resources or the import of parts for manufacturing firms. Oil imports, for example, don't make as significant a difference to the trade balance as is often assumed: They account for only $160 billion dollars, a comparably small sum. Instead, it's the top products of a developed national economy that the United States is importing from everywhere in the world—cars, computers, TV sets, game consoles—without being able to sell as many of its own products on the world market.

"Smaller numbers of unionized workers mean less bargaining power, and less bargaining power results in lower wages."

Unions Can Restore the Middle Class

Robert B. Reich

Much of the rise in middle-class wages and standards of living can be attributed to middle-class workers' involvement in unions, argues Robert B. Reich in the viewpoint that follows. Reich believes that the formation and advocacy of unions resulted in higher wages, improved working conditions, and better health care benefits for working-class Americans. Furthermore, he states that the decline in union membership in all U.S. industry has resulted in a decline in each of these areas and contributed to a shrinking middle class. Reich contends that American workers' desire to form and join unions still exists and should be encouraged if the middle class is to survive the current recession and regain stability in the future. Reich was the U.S. secretary of labor under President Bill Clinton and is currently a professor of public policy at the University of California, Berkeley. He is the author of the book Supercapitalism.

As you read, consider the following questions:

1. Currently, what percentage of private-sector workers are unionized, according to Reich?

2. According to the Department of Labor statistics cited by Reich, what is the difference between unionized workers' salaries and those of nonunionized workers?

3. Why is it so difficult for American workers to form unions today, in Reich's view?

Why is this recession so deep, and what can be done to reverse it?

Hint: Go back about 50 years, when America's middle class was expanding and the economy was soaring. Paychecks were big enough to allow us to buy all the goods and services we produced. It was a virtuous circle. Good pay meant more purchases, and more purchases meant more jobs.

At the center of this virtuous circle were unions. In 1955, more than a third of working Americans belonged to one. Unions gave them the bargaining leverage they needed to get the paychecks that kept the economy going. So many Americans were unionized that wage agreements spilled over to nonunionized workplaces as well. Employers knew they had to match union wages to compete for workers and to recruit the best ones.

Fast forward to a new century. Now, fewer than 8% of private-sector workers are unionized. Corporate opponents argue that Americans no longer want unions. But public opinion surveys, such as a comprehensive poll that Peter D. Hart Research Associates conducted in 2006, suggest that a majority of workers would like to have a union to bargain for better wages, benefits and working conditions. So there must be some other reason for this dramatic decline.

Unions Will Help the Economy

But put that question aside for a moment. One point is clear: Smaller numbers of unionized workers mean less bargaining power, and less bargaining power results in lower wages.

It's no wonder middle-class incomes were dropping even before the recession. As our economy grew between 2001 and the start of 2007, most Americans didn't share in the prosperity. By the time the recession began last year [2008], according to an Economic Policy Institute study, the median income of households headed by those under age 65 was below what it was in 2000.

Typical families kept buying only by going into debt. This was possible as long as the housing bubble expanded. Home-equity loans and refinancing made up for declining paychecks. But that's over. American families no longer have the purchasing power to keep the economy going. Lower paychecks, or no paychecks at all, mean fewer purchases, and fewer purchases mean fewer jobs.

The way to get the economy back on track is to boost the purchasing power of the middle class. One major way to do this is to expand the percentage of working Americans in unions.

Tax rebates won't work because they don't permanently raise wages. Most families used the rebate last year to pay off debt—not a bad thing, but it doesn't keep the virtuous circle running.

Bank bailouts won't work either. Businesses won't borrow to expand without consumers to buy their goods and services. And Americans themselves can't borrow when they're losing their jobs and their incomes are dropping.

Tax cuts for working families, as President [Barack] Obama intends, can do more to help because they extend over time. But only higher wages and benefits for the middle class will have a lasting effect.

The Employee Free Choice Act Would Help Workers Unionize

The decline in union representation has been a major cause of two disturbing trends in our economy: the rise in inequality and the failure of average working Americans to share in the benefits of rising productivity. By reducing the opportunity for employers to intimidate and discourage workers from unionizing after they have reached a collective decision to do so, the Employee Free Choice Act can help restore and spread the benefits that unions bring to workers and the economy. . . .

By requiring employers to accept their employees' choice of bargaining representative, deterring employer violations of the law, and by requiring arbitration of first contracts when necessary, the Employee Free Choice Act will help restore the purchasing power of average Americans and lift the living standards of the 90% of Americans who have endured the middle-class squeeze or have been left out of our economic gains altogether.

Lawrence Mishel, Testimony Before the U.S. Senate Committee on Health, Education, Labor, and Pensions, March 27, 2007.

Unionized Workers Earn Higher Wages with Better Benefits

Unions matter in this equation. According to the Department of Labor, workers in unions earn 30% higher wages—taking home $863 a week, compared with $663 for the typical nonunion worker—and are 59% more likely to have employer-provided health insurance than their nonunion counterparts.

Examples abound. In 2007, nearly 12,000 janitors in Providence, Rhode Island, New Hampshire, and Boston, represented by the Service Employees International Union, won a contract that raised their wages to $16 an hour, guaranteed more work hours and provided family health insurance. In an industry typically staffed by part-time workers with a high turnover rate, a union contract provided janitors with full-time, sustainable jobs that they could count on to raise their families'—and their communities'—standard of living.

In August, 65,000 Verizon workers, represented by the Communications Workers of America, won wage increases totaling nearly 11% and converted temporary jobs to full-time status. Not only did the settlement preserve fully paid health care premiums for all active and retired unionized employees, but Verizon also agreed to provide $2 million a year to fund a collaborative campaign with its unions to achieve meaningful national health care reform.

Difficulty Forming Unions

Although America and its economy need unions, it's become nearly impossible for employees to form one. The Hart poll I cited tells us that 57 million workers would want to be in a union if they could have one. But those who try to form a union, according to researchers at MIT [the Massachusetts Institute of Technology], have only about a 1 in 5 chance of successfully doing so.

The reason? Most of the time, employees who want to form a union are threatened and intimidated by their employers. And all too often, if they don't heed the warnings, they're fired, even though that's illegal. I saw this when I was secretary of labor over a decade ago. We tried to penalize employers that broke the law, but the fines are minuscule. Too many employers consider them a cost of doing business.

This isn't right. The most important feature of the Employee Free Choice Act, which will be considered by the just-seated 111th Congress, toughens penalties against companies that violate their workers' rights. The sooner it's enacted, the better—for U.S. workers and for the U.S. economy.

The American middle class isn't looking for a bailout or a handout. Most people just want a chance to share in the success of the companies they help to prosper. Making it easier for all Americans to form unions would give the middle class the bargaining power it needs for better wages and benefits. And a strong and prosperous middle class is necessary if our economy is to succeed.

> *"We shouldn't be distorting our tax code to benefit a few powerful interests—we should be insisting that everyone pays their fair share."*

The Middle Class Deserves a Tax Break

Barack Obama

In a speech prior to being elected president of the United States in 2008, Illinois senator Barack Obama argues that tax cuts are a necessity for the American middle class and outlines the details of the tax breaks he plans to implement as president. In the following viewpoint, Obama contends that the middle class has suffered from recent tax policy that has allowed the rich to maintain or increase their wealth, while leaving the middle class paying a disproportionate amount of their incomes in taxes. He specifies three ways in which he plans to aid the middle class through modifications to tax policy: a middle class tax break, a tax credit for homeowners, and simplification of the tax code. Obama believes that these three measures will help the American middle class prosper, which in turn will strengthen the nation as a whole. Obama was sworn into office as the forty-fourth president of the United States on January 20, 2009.

Barack Obama, speech on middle class tax fairness, September 18, 2007.

As you read, consider the following questions:

1. Who does Obama believe benefits most from the tax policies initiated under the George W. Bush administration?

2. How does Obama claim a tax cut can help working families?

3. Where does Obama claim the wealth of the nation is rooted?

It's no secret that a fundamental transformation of our economy is taking place. In books and on balance sheets, at policy institutes and around kitchen tables, people are trying to make sense of where the swift and strong currents of globalization are taking us. What we do know is that Americans are living and working in a rapidly changing economic reality.

This isn't the first time this has happened. Time and again, the American economy has undergone upheaval—from slave to free; from agriculture to industry; from peace to wartime, and from wartime to peace. And time and again, the American economy has emerged stronger.

Individual Opportunity Is Essential to a Strong American Economy

The one constant has been the advancement of individual opportunity. There are few principles more basic to our country, and there is none more basic to our economy. We believe that there is a place in the American economy for every American's dream. And we know that when we extend that dream of opportunity to more Americans, all of us gain.

Americans also know that opportunity doesn't come easy. You have to work for it.

Here I think of my father-in-law, Fraser Robinson. He raised his two children with his wife Marian in 1960s Chicago. They faced what other African American families faced at the time—both hidden and overt forms of racism that limited their effort to get ahead. And they faced an additional obstacle. At age 30, Fraser was diagnosed with multiple sclerosis. And yet, every day of his life, even when he had to leave an hour earlier in the morning and rely on a walker to get him there, he went to work at the local water filtration plant while Marian stayed home with the children. And on that single salary, Fraser Robinson provided for his family, sending my wife Michelle and her brother Craig to Princeton.

This is an American story that plays out in millions of families each and every day. It is a story that is shared by the caregiver who is up before dawn and the teacher who never misses the bell; by the trader who works late and the janitor on the night shift. It is the story of a society that values work, and of people who work to create a better future for their families.

Hard Work Is No Longer Rewarded

This story could not exist without a basic social compact in this country. That compact says that if you work hard, your work will be rewarded. That everybody has an opportunity to make a decent living, to raise a family, to give their children the best chance at success, and to look forward to a secure retirement. That people like Fraser and Marian Robinson can give their children the chance to dream bigger, and to reach new horizons.

That social compact is starting to crumble.

In our new economy, there is no shortage of new wealth. But wages are not keeping pace. Workers are more vulnerable to job loss and more worried about retirement. Those Americans fortunate enough to have health care are paying more for it—health care premiums have risen nearly 90% in the last six years. Americans are facing deeper personal debt. From filling up the gas tank to paying for a college education, everything seems to cost more.

This is not just happening by chance. It's not something we can just chalk up to temporary shocks. It's happening in part because of the choices we're making, and the way that we're making those choices. It's happening because we've gone too far from being a country where we're all in this together, to a country where everyone's on their own.

Tax Policy Benefits the Wealthy

Today, I'm going to focus on one aspect of our economic policy where we need to make different choices. Because nowhere is this shift in our priorities more evident than in our tax policies.

Instead of working to find ways to relieve the burden on the middle class, we've developed creative ways to remove the burden from the well-off. Instead of having all of us pay our fair share, we've got over $1 trillion worth of loopholes in the corporate tax code.

This isn't the invisible hand of the market at work. It's the successful work of special interests. For decades, we've seen a successful strategy to ride anti-tax sentiment in this country toward tax cuts that favor wealth, not work. And for decades, we've seen the gaps in wealth in this country grow wider, while the costs to working people are greater.

We've got a shift in our tax values that disproportionately benefits the wealthiest Americans; corporate carve-outs that serve no national purpose; tax breaks that allow companies to stash their profits overseas; a government that's paralyzed when dealing with offshore tax haven countries; an overloaded tax code that's too complicated for ordinary folks to understand, but just complicated enough to work for someone who knows how to work the system.

When big business doesn't like something in the tax code, they can hire a lobbyist to get it changed, but most working people can't afford a high-priced lobbyist. Instead of honoring that core American value—opportunity for all—we've had a system in Washington [D.C.] where our laws and regulations have carved out opportunities for the few.

The numbers don't lie. At a time when income inequality is growing sharper, the [George W.] Bush tax cuts gave the wealthiest 1 percent of Americans a tax cut that was twice as large as the middle class. At a time when Americans are working harder than ever, we are taxing income from work at nearly twice the level that we're taxing gains for investors.

Ensuring Prosperity for All Americans

Talk about this in polite company, and sooner or later you'll get accused of waging class warfare. As if it's distasteful to point out that some CEOs [chief executive officers] make more in ten minutes than a worker makes in ten months. Or, as my friend [American investor and philanthropist, named the second richest person in the world] Warren Buffett put it to me—"if there's class warfare going on in America, then my class is winning."

What Warren Buffett knows is what all Americans have to remember—to get through these uncertain times, we have to recognize that we all have a stake in one another's success. When folks are hurting out there on Main Street, that's not good for Wall Street. When the changes in our economy are leaving too many people behind, the competitiveness of our country risks falling behind. When that dream of opportunity is denied to too many Americans, then ultimately that pain has a way of trickling up.

We welcome success stories here in America. We admire those who have climbed to the top of the ladder. We just need to be sure that the ladder doesn't get taken away from the rest of us. We want a system based on fairness—not special favors.

To steer a course through the change that's taking hold, we have to hold tight to that core principle: that our economy must advance opportunity for all Americans.

The Need for American Tax Policy Reform

My own experience over two decades tells me that when you give people a chance at that opportunity, they will take it. That's what I found as a community organizer on the South Side of Chicago, where we set up job training programs and after-school programs and counseling programs to bring hope to places that had been hurt by change. That's what I found as a state senator in Illinois when we created the state Earned Income Tax Credit so we could put $100 million of tax cuts into the pockets of working families. That's what I've been focused on as a United States senator, as I've worked to expand the child tax credit to include children in minimum wage families, and to close loopholes that shift the tax burden on to working people.

And that's what I'll do as president. Because when it comes to our economy, the American people are not the problem—they are the answer.

I'll restore simplicity to the tax code, and fairness for the American middle class. It's time to stand up to special interest carve-outs. I'll end the preferential treatment that's built into our tax code by eliminating corporate loopholes and tax breaks. We shouldn't be distorting our tax code to benefit a few powerful interests—we should be insisting that everyone pays their fair share, and when I'm president, they will.

And it's time to shed some sunlight not only on companies that abuse the tax code, but also on the secretive offshore tax havens that shelter them. We'll create a list of countries where tax evaders hide their incomes and cost America untold billions of dollars every year. We'll lead the international community to new standards of information sharing. And we'll penalize companies and individuals who use those havens and illegally evade their tax obligations.

If we're going to keep that social compact for a new century, we need a tax code that's fair—a tax code that rewards work and advances opportunity. Every American who is ready to work for their American dream should be able to trust that they have a government that works for them. I'll keep that trust by cutting taxes for working people, homeowners, and seniors, and by simplifying tax filing for middle-class Americans.

Tax Cuts for the Middle Class

First, I'll give a tax cut to working people.

The American people work longer and harder than the people of any other wealthy nation in the world. But their hours are getting longer and their wages aren't getting any higher. Their costs are going up, but their economic security is going down.

When a single mom gets her paycheck, that check gets taxed. When she goes to buy groceries, that purchase gets taxed. When she reaches her retirement, her Social Security benefit gets taxed. Meanwhile, her boss's investments get taxed at a lower rate, and the corporation she works for has all kinds of loopholes built into the tax code because they've got lobbyists in Washington sticking up for their interests.

It's time for that to change. It's time for Americans to have a president in the Oval Office who makes decisions based on their interest, not the special interests.

Let's not forget that even in this era of economic change, our wealth as a nation remains founded on work. I'd reward work by providing an income tax cut of up to $500 per person—or $1,000 for each working family—to offset the payroll tax that they're already paying. At a time when confidence in the American economy is unsteady, this will give middle-class Americans a break, and help them deal with the rising costs of energy, education, and saving for retirement. Under my plan 150 million Americans—and their families—will get a tax cut. And because this credit would be greater than their income tax bill, my proposal would eliminate all income taxes for 10 million working Americans.

Federal Income Tax Is Not Reducing Economic Inequality

The federal tax system is one mechanism for reducing economic inequality. Although higher marginal tax rates on those with very high incomes entail an economic cost, that cost may be lower than for alternative ways of aiding working families, such as trade restrictions or regulations on firms' hiring and compensation practices. However, even while economic inequality has been approaching record levels, the tax cuts enacted since 2001 have sharply reduced progressivity.

Congress has enacted more than $2 trillion in tax cuts since 2001, disproportionately concentrated on the rich. The cuts have almost exclusively applied to the most progressive federal taxes [those where tax rate increases as the amount of money being taxed increases]—income and estate taxes. Only 12 percent of tax units in the bottom income quintile received any benefit, and the average tax savings for that group were about $20 in 2006. Middle-income taxpayers received an average tax cut of $744, barely an eighth of the average $5,790 cut going to the top quintile.

Within the upper strata, the distribution of gains is even more startling. The top 1 percent—the same income group that has reaped most of the income gains in recent decades—got an average tax cut of over $44,000. The richest 0.1 percent—that is, 1 in 1,000 taxpayers—averaged over $230,000 in tax savings.

Leonard E. Burman,
Statement Before the Committee on Ways and Means,
Tax Fairness, the 2001–2006 Tax Cuts, and the AMT,
September 6, 2007.

In so many working families, two parents are working full time, trying to bring up their children, and trying to keep up with so many costs that keep growing while their paychecks don't. This tax credit will strengthen working families by increasing the money in their pockets, and reducing the worry that hangs over so many Americans. And this tax credit will be a particular boost to single working moms, who put in the hours to provide the best opportunities possible for their kids, but struggle to stretch a paycheck that can't cover their growing needs.

Homeowners' Tax Credit

The second thing I'll do to ease the burden on the middle class is provide a universal homeowners' tax credit.

If work is how most Americans seek their dream, a home is how many families realize it. A home is a source of stability, a building block for communities, and the most valuable thing that most middle-class folks will own. But—as has been made painfully clear through the subprime crisis—that source of stability can quickly become the source of economic insecurity. Too many Americans are struggling under the weight of their mortgages. Homeowners need a break.

Today, we have a mortgage interest deduction, but it only goes to people who itemize on their taxes. Like so much in our tax code, this tilts the scales toward the well-off. Only a third of homeowners take advantage of this credit.

I'll create a mortgage interest credit so that both itemizers and non-itemizers get a break. This will immediately benefit 10 million homeowners in America. The vast majority of these are folks who make under $50,000 per year, who will get a break of 10 percent of their mortgage interest rate. For most middle-class families, this will add up to about $500 each year. This credit will also extend a hand to many of the millions of Americans who are stuck in the subprime crisis by giving them some breathing room to refinance or sell their homes. . . .

Simplifying the Tax Code

The final part of my plan will be simplifying the process of filing a tax return for all Americans.

The tax code has become far too complex. Deductions and exemptions are built into the system, but ordinary people don't have the time to figure them out without going to an expert preparer—yet another cost at tax time.

In 2004, the IRS [Internal Revenue Service] estimated that it took 28 hours for an individual to complete her tax filing. According to the IRS National Taxpayer Advocate, "the most serious problem facing taxpayers today is the complexity of the Internal Revenue Code." This past year, *USA Today* had five different professionals add up the tax bill for one working family—and they all got different answers.

It's time to cut through the complexity. When I'm president, we'll put in place a system where 40 million Americans with a job and a bank account who take the standard deduction can do their taxes in less than five minutes. The government already collects wage and bank account information, so there's no reason the IRS can't send Americans prefilled tax forms to verify. This mean's no more worry. No more wasted time. No more extra expenses for a tax preparer.

Making this change would save Americans more than $2 billion in tax preparer fees, more than 200 million hours of work, and an incalculable amount of headache and heartburn.

All of these proposals are about making America's tax code simpler, and making it work better for working Americans.

Promoting Fiscal Responsibility

As we simplify the tax code so that it works for the middle class, we'll have to address shifting costs. Americans are tired of an attitude toward taxing and spending in Washington that is leaving a legacy of debt to our children and grandchildren.

To ensure that we are fiscally responsible, we'll gain revenue by shutting down corporate loopholes and tax havens. We'll also turn the page on an approach that gives repeated tax cuts to the wealthiest 1 percent of Americans even though they don't need them and didn't ask for them. We've lost the balance between work and wealth. I will close the carried interest loophole, and adjust the top dividends and capital gains rate to something closer to—but no greater than—the rates [former president] Ronald Reagan set in 1986.

As we make these changes, we'll be sure to encourage growth and innovation. So we'll exempt start-up companies and small businesses from capital gains to give them an added boost. Because when more Americans tap that well of opportunity, all of us are better off.

Lifting American People and the Country

You know, the truth is, most Americans aren't asking for a lot. They don't need overseas tax shelters or a long list of loopholes. They just want a fair shake. And they could stand a break. Because most Americans have simple dreams. A job. A place to raise their family. A secure retirement. A chance to create opportunities for their kids that might extend a little further than their own.

After all, the wealth of our nation is rooted in the work of our people. In his first State of the Union message to Congress, Abraham Lincoln laid out a core principle: "Capital is only the fruit of labor, and could never have existed if labor had not first existed. Labor is the superior of capital, and deserves much the higher consideration."

It's a simple proposition. That the wealth we earn comes from the work that we do. It's a proposition that is lived, day in and day out, in the homes of millions of working Americans. The steady pursuit of simple dreams.

The American economy is the tally of all of those dreams. Now—at a time of rising costs and rising uncertainty—it's time for polices from Washington that put a little wind at the backs of the American people. Now is the time for us to come together as a nation behind a new compact for the 21st century—one that gives the American people a lift, so they can lift up this country anew.

VIEWPOINT

| *"Taxing or borrowing from the economy and then spending hundreds of billions more through government bureaucracies will have zero effect in promoting economic growth."*

Obama's Tax Break Proposal Is Wrongheaded

Newt Gingrich and Peter Ferrara

In the following viewpoint, Newt Gingrich and Peter Ferrara argue that Barack Obama's tax policy proposals that focus on providing tax credits to low- and middle-income individuals will not provide significant economic relief to these people nor will they spur economic growth. Gingrich and Ferrara contend that the income tax rates currently applied to middle-class individuals and families should be cut, creating a flat rate and increasing the amount of take-home income for these Americans. Calling Obama's plan welfare, the authors worry that his plan offers no incentive for hard work or investment. Gingrich was speaker of the U.S. House of Representatives from 1995 to 1999. Ferrara is the senior policy advisor on Social Security and Medicare at the Institute for Policy Innovation, a conservative public policy organization.

Newt Gingrich and Peter Ferrara, "Let's Have a Real Middle-Class Tax Cut," *Wall Street Journal*, vol. 252, November 20, 2008, p. A19. Copyright © 2008 Dow Jones & Company, Inc. All rights reserved. Reprinted with permission of the authors.

As you read, consider the following questions:

1. Why, according to Gingrich and Ferrara, will the Obama tax credits be ineffective in promoting economic growth?

2. What are the details of the middle-class tax cut proposed by the authors?

3. What percentage of American workers do the authors claim would benefit from their tax proposal?

President-elect Barack Obama is right: America needs a real and meaningful middle-class tax cut. Unfortunately, despite the rhetoric, that is not what his proposals offer.

Mr. Obama's tax plan includes creating or expanding nine or more federal income tax credits mostly focused on low- and moderate-income earners, with an estimated cost of $1.3 trillion over 10 years. These tax credits are provided for certain social purposes, such as child care, health care, education, housing and retirement. Buried amid these is Mr. Obama's purported tax cut for the middle class.

For the bottom 40% of income earners, who pay no federal income taxes on net today, these refundable income tax credits will not reduce tax liability but instead result in new checks from the federal government for the targeted social purposes. That's not a tax cut. It's welfare.

Tax Cuts, Not Tax Credits, Are Necessary

These tax credits will do little or nothing to promote economic growth because they do not reduce marginal tax rates—the rate on the next dollar of income—to provide powerful, meaningful incentives for productive activities such as investment, entrepreneurship, and work. A tax credit is effectively a cash grant that can only affect incentives up to the amount of the grant. Indeed, such tax credits would likely reduce economic growth because the credits are phased out as income rises, and so effectively impose higher marginal tax rates over those income levels.

For a real middle-class tax cut, we should cut the 25% income tax rate that now applies to single workers earning $32,550 to $78,850, and married couples earning $65,100 to $131,450. We should reduce that rate down to the 15% rate paid by workers below these income levels. That would, in effect, establish a flat-rate tax of 15% for close to 90% of American workers.

Marginal tax rates for middle-income families in the 25% tax bracket are too high. Add in effective payroll tax rates of 15% and state income taxes, and these workers are laboring under marginal tax rates of close to 50%. No wonder middle-income wage growth has slowed sharply. Reducing the marginal tax rates for these middle-income earners would lead to income increases for middle-income workers, just as reducing excessive marginal tax rates for higher-income workers did, going all the way back to the Kennedy tax cuts of the 1960s.

Tax Cuts Boost the Economy

This 40% cut in middle-class income tax rates would provide a powerful boost to the economy, greatly expanding incentives for savings, investment and work. This would be much more effective than Mr. Obama's tax plan with its $1.3 trillion in redistributive tax credits, as well as yet another so-called stimulus package based on another $300 billion or more in increased government spending.

Taxing or borrowing from the economy and then spending hundreds of billions more through government bureaucracies will have zero effect in promoting economic growth, as did the failed stimulus package adopted by the [George W.] Bush administration this year [2008].

We could add to this alternative tax proposal an increase in the personal exemption from $3,500 to $7,000. The package would then cut taxes for *all* taxpayers, including those in the lower tax brackets. Of course, reducing the top income tax rates of 28%, 33% and 35%, capital gains tax rates, and the excessive 35% corporate tax rate, would boost the economy even more. But these are the "hate" rates imposed on those who liberals think are too productive, work too hard, and earn too much. Liberals deride these taxpayers as corporate fat cats and "the rich."

Tax Reform That Is Economic Not Social

Fine. Leave those rates for a future initiative. For now, we should focus on the middle-income tax rates that are attractive to cut in the current political climate. This would continue the tax cuts for low- and moderate-income workers Republicans have been adopting for 30 years now.

Because of the highly beneficial effect of these middle-class rate reductions on our economy, and the freedom they would give workers to spend, save, or invest their money as they choose, this proposal would likely enjoy broad public support and present a viable alternative to the liberal social purposes of President-elect Obama's tax credits.

Periodical Bibliography

The following articles have been selected to supplement the diverse views presented in this chapter.

Janet Adamy	"Squeeze for Some in Middle Class," *Wall Street Journal*, July 16, 2009.
Peter Baker	"Speculation Prompts Obama to Renew Vow of No Tax Increase on Middle Class," *New York Times*, August 4, 2009.
Rose Marie Berger	"A Memory of Paradise," *Sojourners*, May 2009.
David Brooks	"The Formerly Middle Class," *New York Times*, November 18, 2008.
CQ Researcher	"Has U.S. Trade and Globalization Policy Hurt the Middle Class?" March 6, 2009.
Peter Ferrara	"Obama's Assault on the Middle Class," *American Spectator*, May 2009.
Stephen J. Rose	"The Myth of Middle-Class Job Loss," *Wall Street Journal*, October 24, 2007.
Harley Shaiken	"Motown Blues: What Next for Detroit?" *Dissent*, Spring 2009.
Wall Street Journal	"The 2% Illusion," February 26, 2009.
David Wessel	"Why Job Market Is Sagging in the Middle," *Wall Street Journal*, October 11, 2007.
Peter Wilby	"The Not-So-Good-Any-More Life," *New Statesman*, April 21, 2008.
Mortimer B. Zuckerman	"The American Dream Goes On," *U.S. News & World Report*, June 13, 2008.

For Further Discussion

Chapter 1

1. The first three viewpoints in the first chapter explore the middle class in terms of income, savings, and standard of living. Clive Crook believes that the middle class is currently better off than at any other time in history due to the widespread ownership of consumer goods such as iPods, microwaves, and televisions. Brian Purnell argues instead that the middle class is in debt and constantly in danger of losing everything because it has borrowed more money than it earns to purchase luxuries. Christian E. Weller contends that the middle class is not spending money on items it doesn't need, but has fallen victim to rising prices of necessities and stagnating wages. Reread these three viewpoints and decide which one you believe most accurately portrays the current situation of the middle class. Incorporate your own experiences or observations to support your viewpoint.

2. Some of the viewpoints in Chapter 1 refer to the early twentieth century American author Horatio Alger and his stories of lower-class boys who ascended to the middle class through perseverance and hard work. Conduct some outside research into Horatio Alger's stories and decide whether you feel these rags-to-riches stories are possible today. Can Americans still move upward into higher classes? Can you think of any contemporary examples of poor Americans moving into the middle or upper class as a result of determination? If yes, describe these examples and compare and contrast them with the heroes of Alger's stories.

3. Reread Pat Barile's viewpoint explaining why he believes there is in fact no middle class and that this class designation is only an illusion to prevent lower classes from organizing and rising up against the upper classes. Do you agree with Barile's view? Based on information from the other viewpoints in the chapter, do you think the middle class has been fooled "into believing that it has common interests with the ruling class," as Barile suggests? Does Barile's designation of only two classes, working and capitalist, leave out other elements of American society? Explain your answer using quotes from the other viewpoints and your own examples as necessary.

Chapter 2

1. Rodney Smith contends that America has forsaken its middle-class appreciation for hard work and sacrifice and is instead overspending its way into debt. Elizabeth Warren and Amelia Warren Tyagi, however, claim that the American middle class is composed of careful shoppers who get better value for their money and save more than their counterparts did three decades ago. Whose image do you think better typifies America's middle class? Explain why, using evidence from the viewpoints.

2. How does Stephen Zacks wage his argument that gentrification of urban areas is a boon for cities? What approach do Kathe Newman and Elvin Wyly use to refute the supposed positive impact of gentrification? Whose rhetorical strategy do you find more convincing and why?

3. Naomi Schaefer Riley maintains that teaching disadvantaged youth to embrace middle-class values can help them to succeed in life and move out of poverty. What values does Schaefer Riley believe she can impart to these young people? Lisa Arrastía claims that pushing middle-class values on disadvantaged youth—who are mostly minorities—is a form of racism. She believes that these young

people are made to feel that their upbringing was not as it should be and that it is best to hold white, middle-class values and opinions. Explain how you interpret this debate and which side of the argument—if either—you believe is justifiable.

Chapter 3

1. The first two viewpoints in Chapter 3 examine the growth of the Latino middle class and its implications for the future. Joel Russell presents statistical evidence showing that the Latino middle class has grown. He also points out that the Latino middle class is benefiting from better business ties with Mexico, Latin America, and South America. Jennifer Wheary, in the second viewpoint, concedes that some growth has occurred, but not on a large enough scale to ensure this population's continued economic growth and security. She believes the government must step in with federally funded programs to stimulate further growth. Examine these viewpoints and decide what steps you think would best foster growth of the Latino middle class. Support your answer with quotes from the viewpoints.

2. Threats to the black middle class examined in this chapter's viewpoints include predatory lending, lack of savings, and poor parenting. Reread the viewpoints by Maya Payne Smart and Kay S. Hymowitz and decide whether you agree with these authors. Is the black middle class really facing a decline? Do black parenting methods deny their children entry into the middle class? Now reconsider the viewpoint by Kris Marsh et al. who argue that the black middle class is not diminishing, rather demographics are simply changing. Which viewpoint do you find most convincing? Could each viewpoint be correct in describing a separate section of the black population? Utilize quotes to prove your point.

Chapter 4

1. Steve Chapman says that critics of the U.S. economy are wrong to assert that the middle class does not have the buying power it once had. He claims that the middle class is far better off today than it has been in the past. Do you agree with this assessment? Compare Chapman's argument to that of Tom Eblen and decide who presents the more convincing analysis of the fortunes of the middle class.

2. According to Lou Dobbs, big business has collared the U.S. government, forcing it to forsake the welfare of the middle class in favor of corporate interests. Gabor Steingart extends this argument by insisting that global corporations have ignored the interests of the American middle class when outsourcing jobs to foreign countries with cheap labor. Do you believe corporate interests are responsible for the supposed decline in the middle class? Agree or take issue with these assertions as you explain your view on the relationship between big business and the health of the middle class.

3. Barack Obama believes that bolstering the middle class is necessary to strengthen the economy in times of fiscal crisis. Read Obama's viewpoint and other recent news about Obama's plans for middle-class recovery. Then, explain whether you agree with Obama's proposals. Do you think strengthening the middle class is the way to restore the U.S. economy, or do you believe that Obama's strategy is misguided? Cite evidence from the viewpoints in this chapter and any outside sources you consulted to support your answer.

Organizations to Contact

The editors have compiled the following list of organizations concerned with the issues debated in this book. The descriptions are derived from materials provided by the organizations. All have publications or information available for interested readers. The list was compiled on the date of publication of the present volume; the information provided here may change. Be aware that many organizations take several weeks or longer to respond to inquiries, so allow as much time as possible.

American Enterprise Institute for Public Policy Research (AEI)

1150 Seventeenth Street NW, Washington, DC 20036
(202) 862-5800 • fax: (202) 862-7177
Web site: www.aei.org

The American Enterprise Institute for Public Policy Research (AEI) is a nonpartisan public policy organization investigating areas such as economics, national defense, health care, and social and cultural studies. The institute sponsors numerous conferences and publishes reports and research on all aspects of American policy. Transcripts of the recent conference "The Myth of the Declining Middle Class" and testimony "The Economic Stagnation of the Black Middle Class (Relative to Whites)" can be found on the AEI Web site. Additional information about the American middle class and other policy issues can be found in the AEI's bi-monthly magazine the *American*.

American Federation of Labor and Congress of Industrial Organizations (AFL-CIO)

815 Sixteenth Street NW, Washington, DC 20006
Web site: www.aflcio.org

The American Federation of Labor and Congress of Industrial Organizations (AFL-CIO) is a federation of fifty-six national and international labor unions representing a wide range of professionals in all fields, from education to labor to the arts. The federation trains workers on methods for improving their local labor unions and ensuring that their voices are heard in discussions concerning workers' rights. Much of the organization's recent commentary on the middle class has focused on its decline and the policy solutions needed to ensure that this class survives the current financial downturn. The AFL-CIO Now Blog provides current information about government action and policy impacting the middle class.

Brookings Institution

1775 Massachusetts Avenue NW, Washington, DC   20036
(202) 797-6000
Web site: www.brookings.edu

The Brookings Institution, a nonprofit think tank, provides policy recommendations stemming from the research conducted by institute scholars. Brookings seeks to ensure the strength of the American democracy, economic and social well-being for the American people, and international cooperation that is open, safe, and prosperous. With regard to the middle class, the institute has explored the impact of current policy and economic conditions. Reports, including "Pathways to the Middle Class: Ensuring Greater Upward Mobility for All Americans," and "The Decline of the White Working Class and the Rise of a Mass Upper Middle Class," can be found on its Web site.

Cato Institute

1000 Massachusetts Avenue NW
Washington, DC   20001-5403
(202) 842-0200 • fax: (202) 842-3490
Web site: www.cato.org

A libertarian think tank founded in 1977, Cato works to advance the principles of individual liberty, free market economics, and peace. Institute scholars produce numerous papers outlining their stances on the economy, national security, and trade. Scholars have analyzed the current situation of the middle class in America in papers and commentaries such as "Middle Class Better Off After Decade of Trade Expansion" and "Falling Behind: How Rising Inequality Harms the Middle Class." Additional information can be found in the institute's publications—the tri-annual *Cato Journal*, the quarterly *Cato's Letter*, and the bi-monthly *Cato Policy Report*.

Center for American Progress (CAP)

1333 H Street NW, 10th Floor, Washington, DC   20005
(202) 682-1611 • fax: (202) 682-1867
e-mail: progress@americanprogress.org
Web site: www.americanprogress.org

The Center for American Progress (CAP) is a progressive public policy organization that seeks to employ modern mass communications techniques to reach a broad audience and promote a philosophy in opposition to traditionally conservative ideals. Specifically, the center advocates for the reestablishment of America as a global leader, the proliferation of clean energy technology to benefit the environment and the economy, economic prosperity for all people, and universal health care. Recent CAP reports focusing on middle-class issues include "Addressing Foreclosures," "The Health Care Delivery System," and "America's Middle Class Still Losing Ground."

Center for Economic and Policy Research (CEPR)

1611 Connecticut Avenue NW, Suite 400
Washington, DC   20009
(202) 293-5380 • fax: (202) 588-1356
e-mail: cepr@cepr.net
Web site: www.cepr.net

The Center for Economic and Policy Research (CEPR) utilizes a two-pronged approach to advance American citizens' understanding of the government and democracy to enable them to make informed choices and encourage their participation. The center first facilitates research on economic and social issues and then presents its findings to the public in a concise, comprehensible manner. Publications relating to the middle class address topics such as the housing market, health care, and trade. These reports and others can be accessed on the CEPR Web site.

Center for Immigration Studies (CIS)

1522 K Street NW, Suite 820, Washington, DC   20005-1202
(202) 466-8185 • fax: (202) 466-8076
e-mail: center@cis.org
Web site: www.cis.org

The Center for Immigration Studies (CIS) has been examining the impact of immigration on the United States and its citizens since 1985. In accordance with its findings, the center advocates for a national immigration policy that ensures immigration does not harm the country or those already living here. CIS believes this vision can be achieved by limiting the number of immigrants entering the country, but providing sufficient aid to those who do. CIS has investigated the impact of immigration on the middle class and has also researched the extent to which immigrants are able to move into the middle class. The center's findings are published in the reports "Immigration and Hispanic Middle Class" and "The Slowing Progress of Immigrants."

Demos

220 Fifth Avenue, 5th Floor, New York, NY   10001
(212) 633-1405
e-mail: info@demos.org
Web site: www.demos.org

Demos, a public policy organization, seeks to ensure that the citizens of the United States are prosperous and actively participate in the democratic process; the public sector's work benefits the people of the country; and the United States takes an active role in international issues. The organization places middle-class prosperity at the center of a successful United States and has focused much of its recent research on the status of the middle class. Publications such as "From Middle to Shaky Ground" and "The State of the Middle Class" can be accessed online along with many other articles.

Economic Policy Institute (EPI)

1333 H Street NW, Suite 300, East Tower
Washington, DC   20005-4707
(202) 775-8810 • fax: (202) 775-0819
e-mail: epi@epi.org
Web site: www.epi.org

The Economic Policy Institute (EPI) is dedicated to providing a voice for low- and middle-income workers in both national and international debates concerning economic policy. The organization publishes its *State of Working America* every two years, outlining conditions faced by working Americans. Additionally, the organization conducts research on issues such as changes in wages, incomes, and prices; health care and education; international trade and economics; and the state of manufacturing and other employment sectors. Recent publications of the institute include "Jobs Picture for August 7, 2009," "How Unions Can Help Restore the Middle Class," and "Tax Cuts Won't Create Jobs."

Heritage Foundation

214 Massachusetts Avenue NE, Washington, DC   20002-4999
(202) 546-4400 • fax: (202) 546-8328
e-mail: info@heritage.org
Web site: www.heritage.org

Promoting policies that espouse the ideals of free enterprise, limited government, individual freedom, traditional American values, and a strong national defense form the basis for the conservative Heritage Foundation's work. The organization has been analyzing the American middle class from a variety of positions, including health care, taxes, and education, since the 1980s. Publications from nearly three decades of research on and observation of the middle class can be read on the foundation's Web site, including "Why the Middle Class Needs School Choice," "The Chicken Little Theory of the Vanishing Middle Class," and "The Middle-Class Welfare Kid Next Door."

Institute for Policy Studies (IPS)

1112 Sixteenth Street NW, Suite 600, Washington, DC   20036
(202) 234-9382 • fax: (202) 387-7915
e-mail: info@ips-dc.org
Web site: www.ips-dc.org

The Institute for Policy Studies (IPS) was founded in 1963 and championed such causes as the anti-war and civil rights movements, focusing during the 1970s on human rights and most recently on international peace and justice movements. While much of the institute's research is conducted on a global scale, its scholars have recently turned their attention toward the plight of the middle class in America. Op-eds, commentaries, and reports by IPS staff can be found on the Web site and include "The Destruction of the Black Middle Class" and "The Unrealized American Dream."

TheMiddleClass.org

40 Exchange Place, Suite 2001, New York, NY   10005
(646) 274-5700 • fax: (646) 274-5699
e-mail: info@drummajorinstitute.org
Web site: www.themiddleclass.org

TheMiddleClass.org is a Web site project of the Drum Major Institute for Public Policy (DMI) dedicated to analyzing current legislation's impact on the American middle class. DMI works to produce reports and studies assessing federal policy annually; however, themiddleclass.org was created to provide up-to-date information about policy decisions as they are being debated to provide the American people with the opportunity to affect the legislation that will most impact their lives. This Web site examines current legislation, gives detailed but accessible summaries of what the legislation covers, and then rates the bills based on the effect they will have on the middle class. Visitors to the site can browse by bill, legislator, state, issue, and pending legislation.

Middle Class Task Force

1600 Pennsylvania Avenue NW, Washington, DC   20500
(202) 456-1111 • fax: (202) 456-2461
Web site: www.astrongmiddleclass.gov

The Middle Class Task Force was created in January 2009 to address the growing concerns of the middle class and to help raise the living standards of the American middle-class family. Vice President Joe Biden is the chair of the committee with other members including the secretaries and directors of major offices within the federal government. The task force seeks to increase education and training opportunities, help establish a work-family balance, improve labor standards, ensure the stability of middle-class incomes, and safeguard retirement funding. The committee's Web site provides updates on its blog and publishes full reports, such as "Why Middle Class Americans Need Health Reform."

World Socialist Web Site (WSWS)

Socialist Equality Party, PO Box 48377, Oak Park, MI   48237
Web site: www.wsws.org

The leadership body of the world socialist movement, the International Committee of the Fourth International, publishes wsws.org, a Web site dedicated to educating the public about socialist ideas and their application worldwide. As a global organization, wsws.org presents an international view of the middle class and their struggles. Reports on the Web site investigate middle-class conditions in China, Germany, Zimbabwe, and Australia, among other countries. Full text of these articles can be accessed online.

Bibliography of Books

Joseph Bensman and Arthur J. Vidich
The New American Society: The Revolution of the Middle Class. Chicago: Quadrangle, 1971.

Benjamin B. Bowser
The Black Middle Class: Social Mobility—and Vulnerability. Boulder, CO: Lynne Rienner, 2007.

Sheryll Cashin
The Failures of Integration: How Race and Class Are Undermining the American Dream. New York: Public Affairs, 2004.

William A.V. Clark
Immigrants and the American Dream: Remaking the Middle Class. New York: Guilford Press, 2003.

Elliott Currie
The Road to Whatever: Middle-Class Culture and the Crisis of Adolescence. New York: Henry Holt, 2005.

James Dale Davidson
The Squeeze. New York: Summit, 1980.

Lou Dobbs
Independents Day: Awakening the American Spirit. New York: Viking, 2007.

Michael Eric Dyson
Is Bill Cosby Right? Or Has the Black Middle Class Lost Its Mind? New York: Basic Civitas, 2005.

John Edwards, Marion Crain, and Arne L. Kalleberg, eds.
Ending Poverty in America: How to Restore the American Dream. New York: New Press, 2007.

Robert H. Frank *Falling Behind: How Rising Inequality Harms the Middle Class*. Berkeley, CA: University of California Press, 2007.

Norton Garfinkle *The American Dream vs. the Gospel of Wealth: The Fight for a Productive Middle-Class Economy*. New Haven, CT: Yale University Press, 2006.

Steven Greenhouse *The Big Squeeze: Tough Times for the American Worker*. New York: Alfred A. Knopf, 2008.

Thom Hartmann *Screwed: The Undeclared War Against the Middle Class—and What We Can Do About It*. San Francisco: Berrett-Koehler, 2006.

Jeffrey M. Hornstein *A Nation of Realtors: A Cultural History of the Twentieth-Century American Middle Class*. Durham, NC: Duke University Press, 2005.

Diana Elizabeth Kendall *Framing Class: Media Representations of Wealth and Poverty in America*. Lanham, MD: Rowman & Littlefield, 2005.

Annette Lareau *Unequal Childhoods: Class, Race, and Family Life*. Berkeley, CA: University of California Press, 2003.

Annette Lareau and Dalton Conley, eds. *Social Class: How Does It Work?* New York: Russell Sage Foundation, 2008.

Bart Landry   *The New Black Middle Class.*
Berkeley, CA: University of California
Press, 1987.

Douglas S.
Massey   *Categorically Unequal: The American
Stratification System.* New York:
Russell Sage Foundation, 2007.

Marina
Moskowitz   *Standard of Living: The Measure of
the Middle Class in Modern America.*
Baltimore, MD: Johns Hopkins
University Press, 2004.

Christopher
Newfield   *Unmaking the Public University: The
Forty-Year Assault on the Middle
Class.* Cambridge, MA: Harvard
University Press, 2008.

Katherine S.
Newman   *Falling from Grace: The Experience of
Downward Mobility in the American
Middle Class.* New York: Vintage,
1988.

Melvin L. Oliver
and Thomas M.
Shapiro   *Black Wealth/White Wealth: A New
Perspective on Racial Inequality.* New
York: Routledge, 2006.

Russ Alan Prince
and Lewis Schiff   *The Middle-Class Millionaire: The
Rise of the New Rich and How They
Are Changing America.* New York:
Currency/Doubleday, 2008.

Charles E.
Schumer   *Positively American: Winning Back the
Middle-Class Majority One Family at
a Time.* Emmaus, PA: Rodale, 2007.

Keith Cameron
Smith   *The Top 10 Distinctions Between
Millionaires and the Middle Class.*
New York: Ballantine, 2007.

| Frederick R. Strobel | *Upward Dreams, Downward Mobility: The Economic Decline of the American Middle Class.* Savage, MD: Rowman & Littlefield, 1993. |

Larry Tye

Rising from the Rails: Pullman Porters and the Making of the Black Middle Class. New York: Henry Holt, 2004.

Alan Wolfe

One Nation, After All: What Middle-Class Americans Really Think About: God, Country, Family, Racism, Welfare, Immigration, Homosexuality, Work, the Right, the Left, and Each Other. New York: Viking, 1998.

Natasha Zaretsky

No Direction Home: The American Family and the Fear of National Decline, 1968–1980. Chapel Hill, NC: University of North Carolina Press, 2007.

Index